The Tax Haven Guide Book

How To Safeguard Your Money, Your Privacy, Your Paradise!

KEN H. FINKELSTEIN
Attorney At Law

◆

BIG ISLAND MEDIA CORP.
USA

Finkelstein, Ken H.

The Tax Haven Guide Book
How To Safeguard Your Money, Your Privacy, Your Paradise!

First Edition

ISBN 0-9665769-0-X

The Definitive Tax Haven Website address:
WWW.OFFSHORELAWYERS.COM

Cover photograph © First Light Associated Photographers
Cover Design by Crystena Jantzen Design

Published in 1998 by Big Island Media Corp.
United States of America

CONTENTS

CHAPTER 1

WELCOME TO PARADISE!

It is one thing to make money ...
quite another to know how to keep it.

◆

Uncertainty, economic and otherwise, surrounds us from cradle to grave. Just prior to publication of this book, that uncertainty relentlessly gripped several notable engines of the global economy:

▸   Japan had sunk to the depths of recession, its banks failing, stock markets plummeting, currency weakening, and unemployment rates escalating to new highs.

▸   The countries of the European Community blindly embraced fiscal uncertainty in their attempt to create a common currency, the "Euro"; an uncertainty heightened by Britain's refusal to relegate its revered pound to the history books.

▸   Hong Kong, Indonesia, and Malaysia, like other once roaring Asian tigers, had been pistol whipped to a barely audible whimper, their economies contracting at an alarming rate, their financial markets melting.

▸   Russia, overwhelmed by the gargantuan task of transforming its society to free markets and democracy after 70 odd years of communist rule, was losing its battle against rampant corruption, social unrest and economic turmoil.

▸   In Canada, reams of red tape and stratospheric tax rates strangled a sputtering economy and provoked currency speculators to hammer the Canadian dollar to its lowest value, relative to the American dollar, in more than 140 years.

But the noose of economic uncertainty did not tighten everywhere. To the contrary, the doom and gloom clutching much of the world was forbidden entry through the doorway to America.

Indeed, for much of the 1990s, U.S. stock markets have been motoring along like a hopped-up Harley Davidson and investors were clamoring to get on for the ride. With the bulls rampaging forward on an unprecedented marathon run, and American stock exchanges repeatedly racking up record highs, there was no denying that Uncle Sam and his constituents were masters of their own financial destiny in these rollicking good times.

However...

Glancing back through the past eighty years of pie charts and wave graphs, it becomes apparent that the law of gravity applies to more than just apples. In the end, what goes up *must* come down. It is ventured that even Alan Greenspan, Chairman of the

United States Federal Reserve Board, would concur.

With this credo in mind, it is envisioned that the cruising Harley (the American economy) will eventually run out of fuel and pull off to the side of the road. Of course, for how long the hog will be out of commission is anyone's guess but it remains inevitable that the tank will one day be empty.

And before the fuel gauge abruptly lights up the "E", it would be wise to prepare for an impending economic downturn by securing your financial affairs - *and part of that preparation may involve going offshore*.

Haven's Gates

Throughout the course of this book, I attempt to dispel the myth there is some sort of complicated mystery behind carrying on business in an offshore tax haven. As well, the notion that exorbitant price tags go hand in hand with setting up offshore structures, such as a private company or a confidential bank account, is laid to rest.

Though at one time tax havens were used almost exclusively by wealthy individuals, the previously guarded gates have now been thrown wide open to welcome anyone seeking legitimate financial protection in a secure environment.

Today, the wealthy continue to make use of tax havens. They have every reason to do so. But now, you are just as likely to catch a fleeting glimpse of the sophisticated James Bond playing blackjack in The Bahamas as you are to see Marge and Homer Simpson dancing an awkward calypso under the enchanting island moonlight.

"Your martini, Mr. Bond."

"Your can of beer, Mr. Simpson."

Ahhh, just another day in paradise ...

The Offshore Surge

Warm tropical breezes and pristine ocean waters are no longer the only attractions to dream-like tax haven islands dotting the global landscape. If you take a peek past the endless beaches lining these alluring get-aways, you will find the sun's rays shining down upon a myriad of banks, investment firms, and trust companies.

Some of these financial houses have been around for decades. Others are relative newcomers. But whether recent or established, home to old money or the *nouveau riche*, these money houses owe their skyrocketing prosperity to more than just smiling fate. They are riding a tidal wave of success generated by a voracious demand for more tax havens, and more of what tax havens have to offer.

Now often referred to as *offshore finance centers,* a term which reflects the inclusion of a diverse range of business services, tax havens have profited from years of uninterrupted growth that seems oblivious to economic malaise infecting other parts of the world.

From individuals to corporations to governments, millions all over the world are entrusting offshore financial institutions with safekeeping more than *half* of this planet's money supply. No, this is not a misprint - more than *50%* of all the world's cash, trillions and trillions of American dollars, is parked offshore!

More than $400 billion of those trillions of greenbacks are guarded by the old grand-daddy of tax havens, Switzerland. Move on over to the Caribbean tropics and find the geographically tiny Cayman Islands counting more than $550 billion dollars divvied up among its hundreds of money houses. Several years ago, the perpetually sunny Caymans surged past the Swiss on the premier money list and now rank in the global heavyweight division, weighing in on the same monetary scale as the most powerful financial centers of the universe: New York, London, and Tokyo.

While the Caymans and Switzerland are two poignant examples of remarkable success, other tax havens are tasting more than a few crumbs from the expanding offshore money pie.

Jersey, an island nation situated between the coasts of Britain and France, has seen its slice grow to the point where it now nudges into the top echelon of the offshore social strata. Jersey's bank deposit levels seem incapable of understanding anything but double digit growth and the country currently boasts more than $100 billion dollars in its banking system.

Tea, crumpets and private banking a mere 50 minutes from London, you say?

Splendid!

IBCs Leading the Way

The popularity of tax havens today is such that any random spin of the globe is likely to stop on a tax haven nation. From Antigua to Vanuatu, and more than 50 other nations in between, tax havens have sprouted up all over the world to meet an ever increasing demand for carrying on business offshore.

This demand is stimulated by several factors, not the least of which is a reasoned desire for individuals to take control of their financial affairs. And one common way of assuming the reins of control involves creating an offshore company, known as an

International Business Corporation (IBC).

Do many people really go to the bother of setting up an IBC? Absolutely - and it is not really much of a bother.

A quick look at the numbers sprinting up IBC registry office ledgers reveals an enormous volume of people who have set forth on the road to financial self-reliance by using an IBC.

Check out statistics from 1997 and you will see that close to *500,000* IBCs were registered in all of the world's tax havens combined, with more than 30,000 IBCs formed in the British Virgin Islands (BVI) alone. That works out to more than 82 companies formed every day in the BVI!

So why are the British Virgin Islands, a Caribbean outpost with a population of little more than 17,000, an irresistible magnet for international business? Why does a popular vacation spot, The Bahamas, run a not too distant second with nearly 20,000 IBCs incorporated last year? Why the exceptional interest in a company formed offshore?

Foremost, it is the *confidentiality* offered by the IBC vehicle that has spurred on this interest and driven its phenomenal growth.

With the information technology revolution swarming all around, and society witnessing a corresponding erosion of privacy rights, individuals are demanding that access to their personal financial matters be blocked from prying eyes.

Without saying too much more at this introductory juncture, an IBC, (i) allows you to seize greater control over your financial affairs; and (ii) shelters your private business from nosy neighbors. The inner workings of IBCs and the confidentiality surrounding their operation are thoroughly discussed in Chapters 2 and 3.

It is this gradual gnawing away at personal privacy that underlies the move towards establishing an IBC or an offshore *trust* within a safe haven; a haven in which banking and investment business is conducted under the protective cloak of secrecy laws.

Offshore banking is comprehensively analyzed in Chapters 4 through 6, and offshore investment trading is reviewed in Chapter 7. Parts of these chapters run through the specific process of *how to* set up and carry on your offshore financial activities.

Owing to the central role that privacy plays in tax havens, Chapter 8 is devoted exclusively to ways in which you may hold your financial affairs under lock and encrypted key.

The offshore trust, one of the most flexible estate planning vehicles, is reviewed in Chapter 9.

◆

As you make your way through *The Tax Haven Guide Book*, ask yourself who has control of your financial destiny. If you think that control is simply a matter of diversifying your asset base and stockpiling cash, then you have answered too quickly.

Make no mistake, while nurturing your nest egg is of utmost importance, it is only the first step. The second and equally critical step involves protecting yourself against life's uncertainties because, as said at the outset, *it is one thing to make money ... quite another to know how to keep it*.

CHAPTER 2

THE IBC PROTECTOR

◆

Diminishing your attraction as a litigation target demands implementing sound preventative measures to protect your assets. One potentially effective measure may involve forming an International Business Company (IBC) in a preferred tax haven *(preferred tax havens listed on page 25)*.

Properly structured, an IBC may provide maximum protection of your rights and your property. Now, before proceeding any further, let me be clear on this one point: using an IBC does not necessarily imply that you are thumbing your nose at the law.

To the contrary, an IBC is a recognized legal entity, something similar to an armored corporate vehicle. Among other uses, an IBC may (i) provide bulletproof financial protection against lawsuits, including those of the pesky variety launched by underhanded persons who recklessly feed the litigation beast by serving up one lawsuit after another regardless of merit; and (ii) empower individuals with control of their financial destiny.

Where's the Justice?

A friend of mine, Maria, visited my office late one Friday afternoon just as I was about to pack it in for the day. Being the considerate person that she is, Maria brought along two steaming cups of coffee, one for each of us, and placed them down upon my desk.

Easing out of work mode and into relaxation, we were casually sipping our coffee and re-hashing the events of the week until Maria, being quite animated in her speech, slung her arm across the desk and smacked her cup of coffee onto the floor. After cleaning it up, I offered to share what remained of my coffee but only on the condition that the cup remain beyond the reach of her wingspan. Amused, she agreed.

Apparently, spilling the coffee triggered Maria's memory and turned our conversation to a court case that I like to call the *hot coffee case,* a story that was recently played up by the press.

The story involved a woman who drove up to the take out window of a popular fast food restaurant to order a cup of coffee. After her order was filled, the woman drove away with the coffee cup resting precariously in her lap. You can probably guess what happened next: the cup was upset and its contents overturned, resulting in burns to parts of the woman's body.

Given our society's ravenous appetite for litigation, it was no surprise when the woman let her fingers do the walking in search of an attorney who would broadcast her injustice to the world. Of course, she did not have to search for very long and quickly found an attorney who would plead her case inside a courtroom and outside to the media hordes.

Now within the hallowed walls of court, the attorney loudly argued that the burns inflicted upon his unfortunate client were caused by the restaurant's reprehensible failure to expressly warn that the *coffee was hot*.

"Okay, here is the part I just do not understand," said Maria in exasperation. "I mean, coffee *is* hot, right? It is supposed to be. That is the nature of coffee. Coffee is hot, grass is green, and summer follows spring."

"Yes."

"But the woman won the case!"

"Right."

"So how can the restaurant be held responsible for their failure to warn someone that coffee is hot? I mean, if it is served cold, then they call it iced coffee, like iced tea, and if it does not say *iced* then we assume it is hot. Who was the judge in this case? Does he live on this planet!?"

Essentially, the restaurant was held responsible because the law said so. Sure, some could find fault with the judge or the jury but, more appropriately, the nature of the legal system as a whole should first be taken to task because decision makers can only work with the tools provided, those tools being "the law."

To many, the tools are flawed because they do not promote *justice,* meaning "fairness" or the "right thing." We have a legal system which seems to engender an ever widening gulf between the *ideal* of justice and the *reality* of the law. Too often, the legal system fails in its responsibility to mete out justice.

But is it failure? To what degree should justice enter into a legal decision? In this particularly absurd case, if justice and the law were connected, then the woman and her hired gun would have been tossed out of the courtroom.

An ornery judge could be imagined to say something like, "So what you are telling me is that you want the restaurant to pay you money for your own carelessness? You are the one who put the cup on your lap, not the restaurant. Case dismissed!"

But in this case, the restaurant was found to be responsible because, like the attorney claimed, it had a legal duty to warn its customers that coffee is hot.

The fact that the restaurant lost the case is bad

enough. What is even worse is that the court saw fit to slap the restaurant with a penalty of several million dollars though the award was later reduced on appeal to *only* several hundred thousand dollars. Is it fair to make someone pay hundreds of thousands of dollars because they did not warn that coffee is hot? Apparently so.

Today, with court awards in the six and seven figure range, and justice sitting quietly on the sidelines, too many shady people dream of dancing dollar signs, file bogus lawsuits, and place their bets in court. Better odds than Vegas, they figure.

And our courts are inhibited by a legal system that does little to deter, and maybe even encourages, frequent lawsuit filers. People are free to roll the dice again and again with the hope that, one day, lucky seven will turn up in the form of victory against a deep pocket defendant.

In the unsettling legal blame game, an alleged victim, of a devious sort, will try to tag fault not on the person who may actually be responsible for damage, but on the person with the most money. If you have money, watch out for the sucker punch lawsuit. You may not know when it is coming but when it does, it will hurt.

So what do you do if you have pockets so deep that unscrupulous rogues out there are licking their chops at the thought of nailing you with a lawsuit? Are there any protective measures you can take?

Foiling the Escape

I wondered aloud whether Maria, being a busy dentist who treats hundreds of people stretched out in her dental chair every year, had considered the possibility that one of her patients might see her as a lawsuit target, a lottery jackpot of some sort.

Maria answered that she saw no reason why she would be put into the same position as the restaurant involved in the *hot coffee case*. I countered that anyone whose work involves dealings with the public, whether it is a dentist, carpenter, teacher, accountant, or anyone else who has socked away some rainy day savings, could be the target of a frivolous lawsuit.

I rambled on until Maria eventually acknowledged the real possibility that she could be sued. Though admitting the risk, she was sure that her dental malpractice insurance policy completely insulated her against all legal claims, whether bogus or legitimate.

Not able to suppress my skepticism, I asked if I could review her insurance policy. One phone call to the insurance company and ten minutes later, the fax machine was spitting out the policy.

While reviewing it, I locked onto the policy's *escape clause.* The so-called escape clause refers to standard language commonly included in insurance policies which allows an insurance company to escape responsibility owed to a policy holder if the holder is determined to be liable under certain circumstances. These specific circumstances were detailed in Maria's policy.

The escape clause in the policy clearly stated that coverage would be denied, "... in the event that a court of law determines that your actions were *grossly* negligent ..."

I gave the policy back to Maria and began explaining the legal notion of negligence. In some circumstances, I said, an act or even a failure to act may be merely negligent. But in other situations, it will be *grossly* negligent. The *gross* part of the equation usually means that the negligence was intentional, mean spirited or even reprehensible. In any event, beyond the usual, "whoops!, my mistake."

"Look," she said in her typically confident manner, "Maybe the policy does not cover gross negligence but that is okay. I have never had any complaints filed against me. I am obsessed with detail and work hard to treat every patient professionally. Tossing all modesty aside, I am extremely good at what I do. Negligence? Highly unlikely. *Grossly* negligent? Forget it. It just would not happen!"

But it might. Mistakes can happen to anyone. And if Maria were to make a mistake and was then sued, her insurance coverage would not kick in if a court determined that she was grossly negligent.

As well, even if Maria's care and treatment was top notch, some scoundrel could whack her with a bogus claim of gross negligence, looking upon her as nothing more than a rich dentist who makes for an appealing lawsuit target.

The bottom line for Maria was that, if someone filed a lawsuit against her, regardless of the validity of the claim, she would have to defend herself in court where her fate and her assets would be out of her control. And there are no sure things in the courtroom except for the fact that, at the end of the trial, the players (attorneys) get paid then move on to the next show, and the extras (clients) celebrate or sulk depending on the decision.

The IBC Protector

With the escape hatch staring Maria in the face, and her assets at risk if the hatch were to burst open, how could she take comfort in the insurance policy? Well, she could not; the protection afforded by the policy was not adequate.

Its terms meant that Maria would be completely

exposed, financially speaking, if her actions were found by a court to be grossly negligent. And if gross negligence were found, odds are that the insurance company would briskly walk, or more likely bolt, through the beckoning hatch.

With the insurance business being a multi-billion dollar industry, you can safely bet that a hefty bottom line does not add up from paying out claims simply because it is the "right" thing to do. If a legal escape from payment is open, well, it sure would be difficult for an insurer to ignore.

"Okay," said Maria. "Now you have me concerned. What would I do if I wanted more protection than that offered by my insurance policy?"

"You have to take action that gives you control of your assets."

"Such as?"

"Well, the first step would be to form an IBC - after that, we would set up an offshore trust." (*Offshore trusts are the subject of chapter 10*).

"This is all legal, right?"

"Right."

"Hmm, maybe you attorneys are not so boring after all; tell me more."

CHAPTER 3

THE NUTS & BOLTS
OF
IBC FORMATION

◆

Okay, here are the nuts and bolts of setting up an IBC. Specifically, this Chapter will review (i) choosing an offshore advisor, (ii) where to set up, (iii) how to set up, and (iv) what it will cost.

Choosing an Offshore Advisor

Alright, admittedly, I am an attorney. And yes, I am now going to tell you why you should use an attorney for your offshore needs. I hasten to add that this is not meant to be a blatant attempt at self-promotion (surely, if I wanted to push my services I could disguise my efforts much better than this!) Seriously, for your own offshore needs, you should understand the advantages of using an attorney.

Advantage number one is privileged communications. This is a concept familiar in the laws of many democratic, common law countries like the United States, Canada, Britain, Australia, and others with similar legal systems. The concept is more properly known as the *attorney-client communication privilege*, and the intent of the privilege is to protect all communications between an attorney and the client which are made during the course of consultation.

The privilege belongs to the client and generally provides that the attorney may not release any information given to the attorney by the client without first obtaining the client's consent.

Strictly interpreted, the client controls the information that may come out of the attorney's mouth. The client may even instruct the attorney not to reveal the fact that the client *is* a client.

This privilege is vital to the open exchange of confidential information. While there are some notable exceptions to the rule, the attorney-client privilege is practically sacrosanct in the eyes of the law. For better or worse, no other profession or occupation is accorded as much legal protection.

A *second* reason to choose an attorney to help set up your IBC is that the formation of any type of offshore structure necessarily involves an understanding of the laws of the tax haven that you choose *and* the laws of the jurisdiction in which you reside. This is legal advice and no other persons are permitted to provide legal advice except for attorneys.

Reason number *three* is that attorneys, as well as accountants, are regulated by their respective professional organizations. These regulations set down acceptable standards of behavior for attorneys and provide the public with recourse against an attorney who engages in bad business practices or violates the ethical codes of conduct to which attorneys subscribe.

Questionable actions can be reported to the local Bar Association, which follow up on complaints filed against a member attorney. Whether or not sanctions would be imposed upon an attorney would depend on the circumstances of the particular case.

The most severe sanction would be loss of license to practice law. With repercussions like that hanging over their head, competent attorneys are sure to fully understand and respect the boundaries of the attorney-client communication privilege.

Accountants also provide the services of an offshore advisor, especially the big international accounting firms. Though they cannot offer the same degree of client communication protection nor provide legal advice, certain accounting firms have gained an expertise in the offshore field. This expertise coupled with the integrity of the accounting profession as a whole make competent accountants a good second choice.

When researching this topic, you will no doubt come across an abundance of "consultants" out there who are neither attorneys nor accountants, nor are they licensed by any regulatory body. Unfortunately, too many of these "consultants" would rightly be called snake oil salesmen; they peddle their wares, i.e., IBCs and offshore trusts, and often dispense wrongful and misleading advice to an unsuspecting public.

If you choose to use the services of a "consultant", save yourself from future migraines by checking out their background and credentials. A little bit of research may save you from buying title to the Brooklyn bridge or depositing your money with a shadowy bank, the kind that mysteriously disappears a few days after receiving your cash.

Where to Form an IBC

Different tax havens offer different advantages and not all are preferred for setting up an IBC. The havens that are most IBC friendly include those listed below, referred to as the *Caribbean 5*:

1.   Turks & Caicos Islands
2.   Belize
3.   British Virgin Islands
4.   The Bahamas
5.   Cayman Islands

The Caribbean 5 offer the following advantages:

►   *Political Stability*

They are British dependent territories or former British territories with a history of democratic and stable government.

▸   *Language*

The language of business is English.

▸   *Bank Secrecy*

Secrecy laws are in force.

▸   *Geographical Location*

They are relatively close to North America, most being in the Eastern Standard Time zone.

▸   *Telecommunications*

Good telecommunications infrastructure is in place.

▸   *Keeping it Quiet*

IBCs need not disclose any financial information nor any other information such as the identity of shareholders, directors and officers; they are not required to file tax returns and are not subject to audit.

▸   *Bare Bones Regulation*

Directors, officers and shareholders may be resident anywhere in the world; other corporations may act in any one or all of these capacities; a single individual or corporation may act as the IBC's sole director, officer, and shareholder; and, except for the Cayman

Islands, formal company meetings are not necessary.

IBCs do not require any sort of minimum capital and shares may be issued for consideration other than cash. Significantly, *bearer* shares may be issued, as discussed in detail on page 33.

Individuals familiar with domestic corporate laws and regulations typically exclaim, "You are telling me that I do not have to inform the tax haven government about the IBC's financial matters? No annual returns to be filed? No disclosure of the names of shareholders?" This minimal burden imposed by tax haven laws is a constant source of astonishment.

I can only guess that the wide-eyed response to minimal regulations results from people assuming that the rest of the world looks much the same as their own backyard. Such an assumption is not surprising if you are used to operating within a highly regulated business environment and are not familiar with more permissive regulations offered by other countries.

When confronted with a more flexible regulatory setting that requires neither reporting nor disclosure, when confronted with more freedom and less restrictions than is the "norm", well, at first the knee jerk response seems to question whether that freedom is real, whether there is a catch.

Well, there is no catch. This is just the way it is in the Caribbean 5.

▸ **No Taxes**

Depending on your circumstances, you may choose to form an IBC in a no tax or low tax haven. And no no taxes means *no* taxes. None. *(see Epilogue for further discussion)*.

▸ **Holding Vehicle**

Similar to a domestic company, an IBC may own all types of assets and undertake business ventures as permitted by law. Assets held may include stocks, mutual funds, real estate, trademarks, or other real or personal property.

▸ **Minimal Cost**

Your cost to set up an IBC depends for the most part on the offshore advisor whom you choose. Generally, you should be able to establish an IBC for no more than $2,000 (USD). This fee should include all company set up costs and assistance with preparing bank and investment trading accounts. Costs are discussed in greater detail starting on page 34.

How to Form an IBC

Start by taking note of the following steps:

▸   ***Choose an IBC Name***

To enhance your privacy, the name should not have any personal connection or obvious tie to you. If your chosen name is available, and it will be unless the name is already taken, the registry will reserve the name for a period of time, anywhere between 30-60 days. In most preferred havens, there is no cost to reserving a name.

There must be a suffix at the end of the IBC name which may be one of the following: Incorporated, Corporation, Limited, Sociedad Anonima, Societe Anonyme, or Gesellschaft mit beschrankter Haftung or their abbreviations being, Inc., Corp., Ltd., S.A. or GmbH. S.A. is familiar in Spanish and French speaking countries while GmbH is known in German speaking countries.

The Turks & Caicos Islands is not typical in that it does not require that a suffix be included with the name. For example, an IBC name may be "Blue Waters". Neither Corp., S.A. nor any other suffix need be attached to the name.

► **Prepare and Submit IBC Documents**

Only two documents are submitted to the IBC registry of your chosen haven. These are the *Memorandum of Association*, which sets forth the objects for which the IBC is formed, and the *Articles of Association*, which detail the bylaws of the IBC.

These are the only documents that remain permanently on record with the tax haven government. From a privacy perspective, it is important to note that only the first shareholders of the IBC, known as *subscribers*, sign their names on these documents.

If permanent confidentiality is desired, it is essential that the Memorandum and the Articles be subscribed to by someone *other* than yourself. Commonly, the IBC's registered agent acts as the initial subscriber. The role of the registered agent is discussed further starting on page 31.

Once the IBC is formed, any transfer of shares or subsequent appointment of officers or directors need not be recorded with the Tax Haven government registry.

Assuming that your name does not appear on any of the IBC documents, then anyone investigating the tax haven's IBC registry will not be able to tie you to the company through the registry. The only name to be found would be that of the registered agent. The significance of this relates to preserving your privacy.

And yes, this is all perfectly legal and in accordance with the laws of the Turks & Caicos Islands and the other governments of the Caribbean 5.

▸ *Incorporation Time*

Once the documents are delivered to the IBC registry, the actual time to incorporate should be between 24 to 48 hours.

Time to incorporate will fluctuate depending on two factors: how many other IBCs are being incorporated on that particular day and, which tax haven is involved. In particular, the Belize IBC registry seems to be lightning quick when registering IBCs while The Bahamas lapses once in a while back to "Island" time, meaning slow, painfully SLOW!

Avoid the first week of January for incorporations; for some reason, this tends to be an extremely popular time for forming IBCs. Could it be that so many people are following through on their New Year's resolution to take control of their financial affairs?

▸ *Registered Agent and Registered Office*

An IBC must have both a registered agent and a registered office. The agent must be a resident of the tax haven where the IBC is incorporated and must be licensed to provide corporate services. Similarly, the registered office must be located in the tax haven where the IBC is incorporated. The office is provided by the registered agent.

Understandably, the governments of the Caribbean 5 give their own residents a chair at the economic table by restricting the pool of registered agents to local residents. Offshore attorneys, accountants, and management companies most often provide the services of a registered agent and a registered office.

For example, if your offshore advisor happens to be an attorney resident in a tax haven, then that attorney may act as the IBC's registered agent. The attorney's office would then be listed as the registered office for the IBC.

If you prefer a domestic attorney as an offshore advisor, then the domestic attorney will retain someone else who is resident in the haven to provide the services of registered agent and office.

Interestingly, there does not seem to be any cost advantage when dealing with an offshore attorney despite the fact that they do not need a middleman to act as a registered agent, as does a domestic attorney.

▸   *Confidential Transfer of Shares*

In contrast to an *ordinary* share certificate, which is

issued in the name of a person or company, a share certificate that is *issued to bearer* does not state any name on the certificate other than "bearer".

To ensure complete confidentiality, the registered agent acts as the initial subscriber to the IBC and transfers their shares to whomever assumes control of the company via *bearer* share certificates.

Once the registered agent transfers their shares to bearer form, only the actual bearer of the shares need know who is the owner. Technically, the bearer is the person who physically holds or possesses the share certificates.

With bearer shares, confidentiality of ownership is safeguarded in the hands of the bearer. As stated earlier, the tax haven government will not be notified of the new shareholder since there is no requirement to file a change of shareholders.

What is the Cost of an IBC?

How much dough do you need before setting up offshore? A basic cost / benefit analysis will lead you to the answer:

Cost of Setting Up IBC + Annual Costs

vs.

Benefits Gained from IBC

Of course, the answer will vary from person to person. Whether going offshore makes financial sense for you depends on your particular circumstances. Consider your circumstances, plug in the elements to the cost / benefit analysis, and you will come up with an answer.

► ***Okay, But What is the Cost?***

I mentioned that an IBC should cost about $2,000 to set up. But what if you pay less than $2,000? Are you getting less for your money? And what if you pay more than that? Will you be getting more?

As with any product or service offered in the free market, cost is a variable dependent on a whole raft of factors. That said, the lowest fee that I have come across for setting up an IBC has been $1,100. This fee is definitely scraping the bottom of the price scale.

At the higher end, I know of a company that was charging $7,500 just to set up an IBC. This is outrageously expensive! Amusingly, this same company recently ran a "special" in which its prices were reduced to $2,000. Well, you know that they are still making a profit at $2,000, so the profit they were making at $7,500 must have been enormous. This is an example of the snake oil vendors whom I spoke of earlier.

▸   *Bits of Wisdom: Buyer Beware*

Because there will be differences in price, product and service, you should shop around before you make the move offshore.

Find out precisely what services are included with the quoted price. The $1,100 price mentioned above included an IBC, all corporate documents, registered agent/office, and a bank account. Not a bad fee!

But, there's always the "but", you were not provided with any legal advice regarding the company or its operations and you were limited to setting up in one country and with one bank. Also, word of mouth told us that service offered after the IBC was purchased was practically non-existent.

Many offshore advisors quote separate fees for each service provided. For example, one fee for the IBC, another for the registered agent, a third for the registered office, additional fees for extra copies of documents, another fee for setting up the bank account, and so on.

Do not be fooled by an advertised fee that is ridiculously low, such as $500. By the time you add up all of the other fees for each separate service, your cost will usually be four or five times the $500.

How do you know that $500 is not your total cost? Ask questions before you reach into your pocket. To be safe, get a quote, in writing, and have it signed by the offshore advisor. Make sure that it's valid for a reasonable amount of time, say 90 days. During this time, you should shop around to compare cost and service with other offshore advisors.

You are in the ballpark if you find a reputable advisor who charges between $1,500 and $2,500. This fee should include the registered agent/office for the first year of incorporation, all corporate documents, 30-60 minutes of no-charge consultation, and free assistance with setting up an offshore bank account and credit card.

Some organizations charge up to $500 *extra* to set up a bank account. Do not be afraid to negotiate the elimination of this fee when you are setting up an IBC. It is a competitive market out there and if your offshore advisor will not lower their fees, walk away and go to someone else.

There is an annual cost to maintaining the IBC, usually ranging from $750 to $1,500. A reasonable annual fee is no more than $1,000. The annual fee should include payment of the tax haven government's annual fee as well as payment for the IBC's registered agent and office.

Other fees might be charged for:

> ▸   *Mail Forwarding*

To keep your privacy intact, any mail directed to the IBC should be sent to the registered office. The IBC's registered agent will then forward the mail to you in a discreet envelope. You would instruct the registered agent as to what address the mail should be delivered. This address should not be your residence if you want to maintain privacy of your financial affairs. Reasonable annual fees for this service range from $175 to $350.

An alternative to mail forwarding is to set up a post office box to which mail from offshore may be delivered. I understand that some American residents who reside close to the U.S. - Mexico border have their IBC's mail sent to a Mexican border town.

> ▸   *Safekeeping of Documents*

This refers to storing the IBC incorporation papers with another person, such as an offshore attorney. Attorneys routinely hold documents on behalf of their clients. As a matter of privacy, this has the advantage of removing the documents from your possession and placing them with your trusted advisor.

◆

After detailing the ins and outs of IBC formation, Maria said that if she were to form an IBC it would be called, "Silver Cap Holdings Corp."

"Once Silver Cap Holdings Corp. is formed, will it protect my money?", Maria asked.

"That could be one of its purposes."

"But the money would have to be offshore, right?"

"Right. For maximum protection, the money should be deposited to an account in the name of Silver Cap Holdings Corp. and the account should be held with an offshore bank."

"If I ask you to tell me about offshore banking, will we be here for a while?"

"Uh huh. More coffee?"

Chapter 4

SHHH! IT'S SECRET

◆

Secrecy is "the" pillar on which the offshore finance industry was built and will always remain integral to its prosperity. Why the secrecy, why the cloak and dagger stuff? Because the nature of the marketplace is that investors demand strict privacy and bank havens are more than willing to cater to that demand.

Rather than sceptically asking why is secrecy needed, how about questioning why anyone else should have access to your financial information; is it really anyone else's business? For those who are already banking offshore, the answer would be a resounding *no*.

Individuals choose to keep their affairs confidential simply because their business is no one else's business unless they decide to make it so. And havens supply the facility to make that choice.

Enforcing Secrecy

Confidentiality, secrecy, privacy - whatever you call it - the critical issue is not the label but whether or not your bank can keep a secret. When assessing the closed-lipped competence of a bank, two issues must be considered *before* your assets take the leap offshore:

▸   Secrecy laws.

▸   Enforcement of secrecy laws.

Is your chosen offshore bank equipped with the legal tools required to keep client privacy? By this, I am talking about whether the bank haven in which the bank is located has passed a secrecy law. The significance of secrecy laws being that they demonstrate the haven government's official commitment to enforcing client confidentiality.

Though there may be slight differences from haven to haven, secrecy laws generally state that those in a position of trust cannot disclose any information concerning a client's affairs without first obtaining that client's consent. Typically, these laws apply not only to banks, but also to trust companies, attorneys, accountants, investment advisers, and others seated in a position of trust.

Banks operating from a secrecy enforced haven can feel secure in pointing to the law as justification for refusing a request to disclose client information. But, if there is no secrecy law or, as an alternative, no entrenched government policy preventing disclosure, as exists in Bermuda, then banks are open to greater pressure from domestic and foreign authorities to lift the lid on confidential information.

While having a secrecy law on the books is a good

start, it is not enough. The law must be *followed and enforced* if it is to be of any consequence. Without compliance, a law is as impotent as a ninety-five year old man sitting limply in a Nevada brothel without his *Viagra* prescription.

To effectively counter any thought of non-compliance with the code of secrecy, two rigid mechanisms are in place:

▸   Built into the secrecy law are provisions that threaten to slap severe penalties against those who violate the law, including heavy fines and jail time.

▸   Aside from a law being on the books, there is the business practicality of the potential for lost business. Meaning that if a particular bank were to violate the secrecy law, then that bank would no doubt scare away potential new clients and would likely lose many current clients as a result of their failure to keep their mouths closed. By association, the haven in which the bank is located would be tarred with a brush of unreliability.

An Amusing Look at Bank Secrecy

Some time ago, I had an amusing encounter with an employee of an internationally recognized bank who did not fully grasp the intent of secrecy laws.

During my conversation with the bank employee, Mr. Jones, I inquired about the bank's current interest rates on fixed term deposits. No big deal, just a little comparison shopping on behalf of a client looking to lock in a few bucks at a good rate of return.

But Mr. Jones stubbornly refused to give out this information. Curious, I asked why. He replied that, since I am not a client of the bank, I had no right to *any* information about the bank!

Baffled, I politely asked to speak with the manager since it was clear that Mr. Jones' confusion was deeply entrenched.

Once I related the story to the manager, he quickly apologized on behalf of the bank and explained that Mr. Jones was a new employee who did not yet fully understand the application of secrecy laws.

Mr. Jones was under the impression that no information should be released to anyone unless they were a client of the bank. Accepting the manager's apology, I then commended him for teaching the bank employees so well, albeit a little too well, in the fine art of silence!

Even if the initial misunderstanding was a bit frustrating, I took comfort in the fact that anyone snooping for information about a client's account may face a similar blockade.

Violating Secrecy: Cases on Point

Say that a haven government has secrecy laws in place and those laws are strictly upheld for many years. One day, however, the secrecy law is violated; client information is improperly disclosed.

Should the offending bank be trusted any longer to keep secrets? Can the bank haven in which the bank is located be trusted to enforce its own secrecy laws?

Well, two of the noted big boys of bank havens, Switzerland and the Cayman Islands, have both experienced this unpleasantry and it is worthwhile examining exactly what caused the secrecy veil to be pierced.

▶   *Switzerland*

The Swiss are as renowned for their banks as for neurotic adherence to the 24-hour clock and a history of sitting on the political fence. For more than 60 years, Swiss banks firmly enforced client secrecy to the letter of the law. During this time, their reputation as trustworthy bankers had become legend among private investors.

But yesterday's legend has been smudged by today's reality: In 1997, Swiss secrecy laws were violated. The result being that the vaunted Swiss reliability was placed in serious doubt.

In order to understand the reasons for lifting the veil of secrecy, a brief look into the background of this matter must first be examined.

In the years leading up to, and during, the Second World War, Swiss banks collaborated to some degree with the Nazis. To what degree they were involved is a matter to be determined by historians, politicians, and others involved with digging up the facts. Political history is a realm I do not intend to enter in this book.

It is sufficient to know that Swiss banks assisted the Nazis with depositing vast fortunes of gold looted from central banks of conquered countries and from individual victims. Some of this gold was laundered into hard currency for the purpose of funding the Nazi war machine, while other remaining ingots were held in Swiss bank vaults.

Also on deposit with Swiss banks were millions of dollars in savings accounts belonging to eventual WWII victims. To no avail, the families of these victims tried for years to break through the Swiss wall of silence and gain access to these funds.

Eventually, certain powerful political groups, including high profile members of the United States government, took up the fight against the Swiss banks on behalf of the families of WWII victims. During the first round of the bout, a list of names of persons who set up accounts during the war years was requested.

The rationale underlying the call for disclosure was that the victims' relatives have a moral right to claim these funds and, in these particular circumstances, Swiss secrecy laws should not act as a barrier. If the barrier was not removed, the money would wrongfully remain with the Swiss banks.

In round two, the Swiss balked at the request to raise the confidentiality curtain with bank secrecy laws being invoked as justification for strict adherence to confidentiality. Morality and fairness, argued the Swiss, were not proper issues in this matter. The only issue was maintaining client trust.

After almost 60 years of hush hush privacy between the banks and their clients, the Swiss were not about to voluntarily open their secret bank records to the world.

Fully realizing that polite requests for cooperation were being rebuffed time after time, the Swiss adversaries unleashed a new and powerful jab aimed squarely at the Swiss glass chin.

Leverage being the name of the game, the chairman of the U.S. Senate and Finance Banking Committee, who happened to hail from the State of New York, questioned whether Swiss banks should be allowed to carry on business in New York, *the* financial capital of the world.

Ouch, that hurts! Knowing they were on the ropes, the first beads of Swiss sweat dribbled down. The bank's bottom line was now at stake. If the privilege accorded to Switzerland's largest and most prestigious banks to operate on Wall Street was revoked, well then, that meant that their reputations and profits could sink right into a Bronx pothole.

The threat of such drastic action persuaded the Swiss to relent, but only slightly and certainly not enough to satisfy their detractors. So the pressure did not ease. California, among the world's ten largest economies, and no financial slouch, was added to the pot of threats stirring against the Swiss. Now, the nation's most populous state had stepped on side with New York and had agreed to bar Swiss banks from carrying on business.

Down for the count, the Swiss released the names of account holders.

Does this violation by the Swiss of their own laws mean that their banks can no longer be trusted to protect client confidentiality?

No, not necessarily. Under ordinary circumstances, 60 odd years of history tells us that the Swiss would follow their secrecy laws. If nothing else, they are an integral part of Swiss culture and a part of their independence; a part which the Swiss wish to protect, as evidenced by their steadfast opposition against disclosure.

As the second most popular financial haven, in terms of dollars on deposit, and with banking being an indispensable part of the Swiss economy, Switzerland wants the world to know that its secrecy laws remain in force.

Why? Because the bottom line matters.

▸   *Cayman Islands*

Like the Swiss, the Caymans also caved to foreign pressure and violated their own secrecy laws.

Back in the early 1990's, the U.S. government was investigating one of its citizens for alleged tax evasion, among other matters. Uncle Sam wanted to know the location of this individual's assets, which were reportedly significant.

Snooping around, they found reason to believe that substantial cash deposits were held by this individual with the Cayman Islands branch of The Bank of Nova Scotia (BNS).

Uncle Sam submitted a request to BNS for details concerning business carried on by this individual. In response, BNS denied the request citing the Cayman's bank secrecy laws as justification. Any compliance by BNS would result in a violation of Cayman laws and BNS held its allegiance to the Caymans, for the moment anyway.

The U.S. shot back with an ultimatum, the gist of which follows:

"Sirs," they began, "For every day that you refuse to comply with our information request, your branch located in Miami will be fined $25,000. And the fines may continue indefinitely as there will not be any maximum."

It did not take very long for the fines to pass the one million dollar mark. At this dollar high mark, BNS started to rethink its position. Eventually, in the face of financial penalties climbing higher and higher, BNS capitulated. Allegiance was no longer sworn to the Cayman secrecy laws but rather to the dollar, BNS' dollars that is.

The Cayman's secrecy law was chucked out the window, client privacy was nudged aside, and the fines stopped piling up. It goes without saying that, in this case, the biggest loser was the individual under investigation, not BNS.

▸   ## *The Bottom Line*

The BNS story is similar to the Swiss in the sense that morality never entered into the bankers' equation. The bank bailed out and left its' client stranded when the U.S. government took too big a bite out of its bottom line.

In both cases, each bank had operations in the United States, operations which fell within the legal jurisdiction of the U.S. government. What this meant was that the U.S. government had leverage: they could fine the banks or even close down their operations.

As discussed below, some countries may not have the option of whacking foreign banks with monetary penalties. As an alternative, these countries play the less effective *morality card* with the intent to convince their residents that bank havens are not in their best interest.

Chancellor Kohl's Big Stick

German residents are fleeing with their money to banks located in Luxembourg, Liechtenstein, and Switzerland, three reputable tax havens that just happen to share a border with Germany. In Germany, as in other high taxed countries, dodging taxes is reportedly something of a national sport.

To dissuade those who run with their money beyond the border and then fail to pay taxes on earned income, Chancellor Kohl's German government has implemented the "snitch" law.

The aim of the so-called "snitch" law is to enlist German residents to walk arm in arm with the government in its effort to thwart evasion. Meaning that the government offers money to those who provide them with reliable information regarding a German taxpayer who fails to report income earned from offshore sources.

Whether or not this approach has influenced Germans not to park their money offshore is anyone's guess. However, other actions taken by the German government suggest that the snitch law, by itself, has not been enough of a deterrent.

Fully aware of the inclinations of some of its residents, the government now relies not only on snitches to inform on their neighbors, but also conducts raids on foreign banks operating in Germany. These banks often hold information concerning German account holders who have accounts in offshore countries, such as Luxembourg.

The government then compels the German-based foreign bank to release vital information, namely the identities of German residents who hold accounts with an offshore branch of the same bank.

After a few successful raids, some of the account holders finally woke up: they closed their accounts held with any foreign bank that has a branch office, affiliate, or subsidiary in Germany.

Next, accounts were opened with an offshore bank that does not have any operations in Germany. Now, these account holders were beyond the long arm of German law since the government has no right to step into a foreign country and demand information from a foreign bank that has no business ties to Germany.

But the winner in this see-saw battle has yet to be declared. During deliberations, determined authorities came up with a new strategy: in addition to targeting foreign banks carrying on business in Germany, they would now expand their hit list to include home grown banks that maintain operations in offshore countries.

This new strategy was activated in June, 1998, when some 300 tax inspectors raided the country's biggest financial institution. What were the men in gray suits scrounging around for? It turns out to have been a search for records showing interest income paid to German residents who hold bank accounts with branch offices of this particular financial institution located *outside* of Germany.

Not too wisely, it seems that foreign branch client records of this financial institution were held in

Germany rather than in the country where the branch was located. The records would have been protected if they were held in an offshore country such as Luxembourg.

So far, the result of these raids has been twofold: first, the German government caught some tax evaders in its massive net and collected taxes owing; second, the hurdles were raised once again for those who played the sport of tax dodging.

The Tax Authority: What are They Thinking?

Unfortunately, like too many other countries, the tax policy brains in Germany seem quite muddled at times. Instead of wasting enormous amounts of time, resources, and taxpayers money on raids, they should be REDUCING TAXES in their effort to combat tax evasion and collect tax money owing.

It is a shame that other politicians do not follow the lead of ex-British Prime Minister Margaret Thatcher. Shortly after she took office, taxes were substantially reduced. What happened? The British government collected *more* revenue with *lower* taxation rates than they did in the years when the marginal tax rate approached 80%!

Does this make sense? Absolutely!

The British experience is strong evidence that too heavy a tax burden leads to a silent but active revolt among those who decide to take matters into their own hands. As well, it appears that a fair tax load will see these same people playing by the rules of the taxman.

Sure, there will always be an underground economy and there will always be some folks operating their lives on the fringe, completely outside of the social/political system. But it becomes scary, for society as a whole, when significant numbers of people walk away from their societal obligations.

Paying taxes is one of those obligations and tax dollars are intended to serve the common good by financing our social/legal/environmental/commercial infrastructure. But when too many people are not paying their share, societies' institutions feel the pinch and soon start to decay. And we all suffer.

So the questions must be asked: are too many individuals not paying their share of the tax load? Is it these same individuals who are making the move offshore? Why is this societal obligation being ignored? Chancellor Kohl, are you listening? As much as it may haunt you, Margaret Thatcher is talking.

A Revolutionary Idea - Reducing Taxes

Tax authorities worldwide fear the flight of capital from their own countries to offshore havens. Once money is nestled within haven vaults, it is often impossible to track the funds, let alone lay claim to them.

So, the taxman takes preventative measures to block the transfer of funds from within their jurisdiction to the outside. As seen with the "snitch" law, these measures commonly include the weapon of moral persuasion to convince people that offshore havens are somehow sinister.

The Canadian government, for example, will soon pass a law requiring any resident with more than $100,000 in assets located outside of Canada to disclose this fact when filing their tax returns and to provide specific details related to the asset type and location.

The government hopes that the threat of onerous fines for failure to comply with the new law will convince people to keep their assets at home or, if their assets leave the country, then to disclose this information to the taxman.

Will the law be effective? Has the "snitch" law served its purpose? Probably not.

It seems that anyone who discloses this information to the government has nothing to hide and, in such cases, the government will simply be adding to its already overloaded information banks. Those who do have something to hide are unlikely to disclose information anyway, and the government will be no further ahead since they will still not have any means of accessing information concerning offshore activities.

Instead of enlarging an already bloated bureaucracy by passing more laws, hiring more tax inspectors, and creating more forms to be filed, how about copying a page or two from Mrs. Thatcher's policies, i.e., tax reduction. Why not tackle the root of the problem rather than wasting considerable time and vast amounts of taxpayer money on a law that may serve little purpose?

But that is just my naive two cents worth. Some political leaders obviously disagree with this modest leap of logic and might even say that this reasoning is worth far less then two cents. So be it.

◆

During the late spring of 1998, the member nations of the Organization for Economic Development and Cooperation (OECD), led by the U.S., U.K., France, and Germany, put the issue of tax evasion on their agenda.

They talked about preventing evasion through more restrictive enforcement of monetary reporting requirements on individuals and financial institutions alike, and protecting their right to impose higher taxes on their residents.

But with trillions of dollars already parked in tax havens, some of it possibly put there by the very politicians trying to restrict their use, you might think that these high tax countries would stop proposing the same ineffective solution to a long time problem. Maybe the political leaders would, instead of drudging up their time worn solution of harsher financial penalties, analyze the reasons why people are taking their money offshore and then suggest alternatives.

Maybe they would at least try to comprehend why, for example, close to half a billion dollars is protected by the Turks & Caicos Islands, a stunningly serene and beautiful Caribbean country of just 15,000 people. That is a lot of dough for a tiny Caribbean country that offers nothing much but perpetual sun, sand, beach, resorts, and no taxes ... oh, did I say paradise?

Unfortunate though it may be for society as a whole, the result of more restrictive government measures is that those who can are not waiting for the next election to dump wasteful and ineffective politicians.

Rather, they are taking matters into their own hands by voting with their feet and their wallets.

Those left behind will be worse off since, not only is individual talent and money deserting the country at a startling rate to no tax and low tax countries, but they are taking their future tax dollars with them.

The Case for Unveiling Secrecy

Most bank havens will assist foreign countries with the investigation of individuals who are suspected of laundering money from drug proceeds, military arms sales, or other serious crimes. And so they should.

Assistance has been formalized by agreeing to the terms of the Mutual Legal Assistance Treaty (the "MLAT"), an agreement executed between havens and other governments, notably the United States and the United Kingdom.

The MLAT is an agreement about fair play. Essentially, it says, "Okay, you want to have your bank secrecy laws, well, we may not like it, but go ahead, have your secrecy laws. But we have to draw the line somewhere ..."

This line is drawn in the form of haven governments cooperating with OECD countries by disclosing information about individuals who are involved with serious criminal activities.

Typically, havens do not list tax evasion under the heading of serious criminal activities. The reasoning goes something like this: if there are no taxes imposed by the haven, then the concept of tax evasion simply does not exist. No one can evade taxes because there are no taxes required to be paid.

Recently, the OECD proposed that havens extend their agreement to cooperate when residents of OECD countries are being investigated in their home countries for tax evasion and it is suspected that they hold assets offshore.

No tax haven has yet agreed to this proposal but some may be more subject to pressure than others. For example, many Caribbean islands are still British colonies and rely on a certain amount of financial assistance from the UK government.

Could it be that this insistence on disclosure of information in tax related cases is just a ploy by the UK government? Maybe their intent is to force the hand of the Caribbean colonies to cut their ties with London and opt for the road to independence thus lessening London's foreign financial aid package.

What about the Channel Island outposts of Jersey, Guernsey, and Isle of Man, each of which are within an hour's flight of London? The British government recently ordered a top to bottom review of financial regulations, procedures, and activities in these havens.

For the most part, these islands are independent from London in that they do not require financial assistance. With this in mind, could it be that London is taking the first step toward closing the doors to offshore business in these jurisdictions? Apparently, pressure from other major European countries, such as Germany and France, is growing to outlaw offshore jurisdictions located within the borders of Europe.

Practically speaking, the U.K. and U.S. could shut down the operations of most havens overnight. How? Simple, really: as the U.S. has done with Cuba, they would forbid Americans from ever visiting or doing business with the offshore country in question, and then do their best to persuade other OECD countries that it is in their interest to follow the lead of the U.S. Since these countries have a strong interest in collecting tax revenue, there may not be much hesitation when deciding whether to follow the U.S.

Has a shut down ever been attempted?

No.

Will it be attempted?

Probably not.

How can I be sure?

Because some of the most influential and powerful political and business leaders in the world make use of bank havens. And it is highly unlikely that these people would take any action that would harm their own financial position.

And because the world's richest banks, who are among the world's largest employers and play an integral role in global capitalist markets, rake in tremendous amounts of cash in bank havens - hanging an "out of business" sign would blast a gaping hole in the bottom line of these banks and endanger the stability of global markets. Shutting down haven operations would cut sharply the wrong way against the self-interest of banks and the world's major financial markets.

So it is that bank havens will live long and prosper.

Chapter 5

WHERE IN THE WORLD IS
YOUR
OFFSHORE BANK?

◆

In the context of choosing a bank haven, it would be helpful at this point to repeat parts of the conversation in which Maria and I were engaged. Following this interesting little story, the factors that must be considered before choosing a bank haven will be discussed.

The Nutty Patient

"Imagine," said Maria, "that I have formed Silver Cap Holdings Corp. in Belize and dumped some cash in a bank in Belize. A few months later, an old patient of mine walks into my office, greets the receptionist and loudly announces that he is not there for his annual dental check-up. Instead, the only cleaning he wants is to clean out my offshore bank account as payback for the pain and suffering I allegedly caused him during a visit several months ago.

Say that the guy is a nut case and, like you mentioned, he sees me as a deep pocket lawsuit target. At this point, he has not sued me. Before he goes to the expense of filing a bogus lawsuit, he is trying to pressure me into paying him off so that he will keep his mouth shut about my offshore business and not take me to court."

"I have him tossed out of the office and then call you to ask how I should get rid of him."

"Okay."

"So, how do I get rid of him?"

"First, is he bluffing about your offshore account or does he actually know something?"

"Say that he knows something. My partner, who talks too much, heard me mentioning my offshore business to you on the telephone one day and she then repeated what I said to her assistant. The nut case was being treated at the time that my partner blabbed and he assumed that my partner had accurate information."

"So what does your nutty patient really know?"

"He knows that I have a company and a bank account in Belize."

"And you simply want to protect the confidentiality of your offshore business?"

"Right. I want some money offshore that I will invest and fulfill my tax obligations on whatever money is made. But I do not want other people to know about my business."

"Alright," I said, "Let me take it from here. Imagine that, as you said, your patient has no valid claim against you and is just harassing you in an attempt to extort some easy cash. However, you refuse to negotiate with the guy.

Angry, he decides to go one step further and gather specific information about your offshore business which he intends to use as ammunition in his lawsuit against you. He hires an attorney in Belize who searches the Belize IBC Registry to verify the owner of Silver Cap Holdings Corp.

But the IBC Registry reveals no information except for the name and address of the IBC's first shareholder and director, who is listed as another Belize attorney, the one who assisted with the set up of Silver Cap. Once the attorney transferred his shares, the identity of the new shareholder was forever cloaked since the IBC is not required to inform the Registry of any change of shareholders. Therefore, whether or not you actually own the IBC cannot be confirmed by the Registry.

Also, the Belize attorney who acted as the IBC's first shareholder and director will not disclose any information about Silver Cap because of the attorney-client communications privilege that exists between you and him."

"Assume," said Maria, "that the patient is persistent. He tries to tie me to the IBC by finding out where

Silver Cap does its banking because he is sure that I will be listed as an authorized signatory on its bank account."

"Okay. Since he does not know where the IBC banks, he would have to check every bank in Belize. Given that the patient does not know the name of your IBC and the account is in the name of Silver Cap, he would have to obtain a list of every IBC account and review the documents for each account for a listing of the authorized signatories. No small undertaking!

Add to that the fact that Belize has strict secrecy laws which forbid the release of this information without the client's consent. Anyone who were to assist the nutty patient would be risking financial penalties and jail time."

"Seems airtight. Still, what if he enlists the help of a crooked bank employee, finds the account, forgets about bringing a lawsuit against me but tries to siphon the money out of the account?"

"If you think that this is a possibility, then as soon as the patient mentioned your offshore account, you would transfer the funds to another bank in another country. Your patient, whom I imagine has found another dentist by now, will likely give up after searching through the Belize banks. If he cannot find your money in Belize, well, then he has the rest of the world to search if he has no other leads as to where your cash may be."

"So I lessen the risk that my privacy could be violated by holding assets with more than one bank?

"Yes. Any more questions?"

"There will be."

Choosing a Bank Haven

With a population of 30,000 people and close to 600 financial institutions, Cayman Islands residents could be forgiven for having difficulty in deciding which finance house should hold their money.   And the houses could rightfully whine to the local financial regulatory authority about the fierce competition created by their sheer numbers.

Surely, the whining would be justified if the finance houses served only Cayman residents. If that were so, and if a proportional number of residents carried on their financial transactions with each of the financial institutions, then a mere 50 customers would frequent each of the houses! Unless the customer list included a few oil sheiks or software titans, odds are that the banks would struggle to stay afloat.

The reality, of course, is that the country's money houses are not lacking for business, not at all! Profits have been rocketing skyward for several years owing to customer lists that include both Cayman Island locals as well as residents of the rest of the globe.

American dollars, German marks, British pounds, Japanese yen, Swiss francs, Italian lira, Canadian dollars, Dutch guilders ... all nationalities are migrating to these tiny tropical islands.

Without doubt, the Caymans are a good choice for offshore cash custodian but they are not the only game in town. Other significant bank havens are attracting their fair share of foreign funds including: The Bahamas, Bermuda, Guernsey, Jersey, Luxembourg, and Switzerland, as well as smaller centres such as Barbados, British Virgin Islands, Cyprus, Gibraltar, Isle of Man, Mauritius, and the Turks & Caicos Islands.

▸   ***Bank Secrecy Laws***

As discussed in detail in chapter 4, it is preferable for the haven to have passed a specific law covering bank secrecy. However, if there is no secrecy law, it may be sufficient if the haven has a history of enforcing bank secrecy and, by its actions, the government's commitment to enforcement is made clear.

► *Political Stability*

Political stability is practically non-existent in dictator controlled regimes and developing states that have only recently embarked upon the road to democracy.

In these countries, your money may be here today, gone tomorrow. It is this political, and resulting economic, uncertainty which persuades individuals to hedge their risk by transferring funds to a safe bank haven.

Indonesia provides an example of a politically unstable country where residents would have been wise to hold assets in a safe haven *before* the breakout of political and economic havoc.

The Indonesian mess culminated with the unceremonious dumping of President Suharto during the spring of 1998. Unfortunately for its residents, damage to the country had already been done prior to Suharto being forced from office. With the drastic devaluation of the Indonesian currency, and the vast majority of the population not holding assets in any foreign currency, the middle classes suddenly belonged to the poor.

And the fate of the now ex-President? Well, like other deposed Third World dictators before him, you can be sure that during his nearly three decades of rule, Suharto squirrelled away a few billion dollars, give or take a million, for a rainy day ... or an abrupt end to his dictatorship.

If he kept all of his money in Indonesia and his assets, including cash, in Indonesian currency, then he had his head in the sand. If he had astute advisors, then it is likely that he prepared for his political demise by stashing some cash in a politically safe bank haven.

Predictably, residents of Indonesia and other politically unsteady countries who anticipated a down fall in fortunes were converting local money to historically strong currencies and then sending it off to safety.

Your chosen bank haven must be politically stable. If not, your money is at risk.

▸ *Financial Instability*

While political instability may be the primary motivation driving residents of emerging democracies to transfer their assets offshore, in established western democracies, it is fiscal and financial instability within our own banking system, whether real or perceived, which causes individuals to search for a safer alternative.

American residents remember the Saving & Loan crisis that exploded in the 1980s: billions of dollars held on deposit were lost, life savings were wiped out, and the Federal Deposit Insurance Corporation covered only a fraction of the losses. This meant that the U.S. Government, i.e., the American taxpayer, was stuck with a sky high bail out bill.

The decade of greed, the 1980s, was also a wake up call to habitually complacent Canadians. Despite federal banking regulations purportedly imposed to protect depositors from loss, Canada witnessed its first bank failure in almost 40 years. Now, Canadian banks could no longer claim to be as solid as Rocky Mountain ice caps.

Across the Atlantic Ocean, her majesty's loyal subjects did not escape unscathed from financial scandal. The early 1990s witnessed a centuries old British bank come tumbling down as a result of enormous investment trading losses apparently racked up by a single rogue trader.

Although the trader may have been directly responsible for the losses, it was necessary for upper management to first give the trader authority to bet the farm on risky investments. A model of fiscal stability and prudent financial practices this bank was not.

➤ ***Deposit Insurance***

Since deposit insurance schemes, such as the Federal Deposit Insurance Corporation (FDIC) in the U.S. or the Canadian Deposit Insurance Corporation (CDIC) in Canada, are not commonly found in offshore countries, reducing risk exposure requires that you bank in one of the more well established havens with a major bank.

The Isle of Man is the only tax haven of good repute that offers deposit protection. The protection is quite limited, however, in that only 75% of the equivalent of a maximum of about $30,000 (USD) is insured.

➤ ***Currency Controls***

Stay away from any country that restricts the movement of money, either in or out. Banking in a country where regulation is king places your money at permanent risk of being frozen or even seized at the whim of government.

➤ ***Language Spoken***

If English is your spoken language, you should bank in a country where the official language, or at least the language of commerce, is English.

This is a practical matter. If the bank account is set

up in a country where English is not commonly spoken, you place yourself at greater risk of miscommunication between yourself and the bank.

Though there is a reduced risk of miscommunication when both you and the bank communicate in English, that risk still remains, especially in some of the Caribbean countries.

I have no intention of taking pot shots at the hundreds of Caribbean based banks; there are many excellent institutions in the Caribbean havens. But, bear in mind that employees of some Caribbean banks move at a different speed, a much, much slower speed, than North Americans.

Often, the bank staff are poking around in first gear and you have downshifted to fourth since your morning caffeine jolt. If this is the case, it will be difficult for the staff to comprehend your need for expediency in carrying out banking transactions.

To some, this may not be much of a concern. To others, it is a source of frustration and annoyance. To avoid this problem, consider your advisor's advice as to which banks have been in the sun a little too long.

▸ ***Communications***

The bank haven should be served by at least one major airline, provide daily postal service, courier service by at least one of the major courier companies, and a good telecommunications system.

Note that the telecommunications infrastructure of some haven countries have a limited number of telephone lines and are prone to occasional delays or interruptions.

Of course, some communication problems cannot be controlled. For example, a hurricane during the summer of 1997 shut down business in several of the Caribbean countries for a few days, including The Bahamas.

► ***Geographical Location***

Many individuals lean toward banking in a country that is relatively close to their own place of residence or business. The primary reason for this preference is similar time zones. If you are in Boston or Toronto and your offshore bank is in the Turks & Caicos Islands, there is no time difference since both places are on Eastern Standard Time. This makes it convenient to contact your bank.

By contrast, a resident of Los Angeles who sets up a bank account in one of the South Pacific havens, such as Vanuatu or the Cook Islands, faces a time difference of as much as 19 hours! To say the least, a time difference like that can wreak havoc with your sleeping patterns and be downright inconvenient.

◆

Now that you have the skinny on choosing a bank haven, the next step is learning how to set up a bank account.

Chapter 6

HOW TO SET UP
YOUR
OFFSHORE BANK ACCOUNT

◆

The Way of Capitalism

Why have so many financial institutions established themselves in bank havens?

TO MAKE MONEY!

As Luxembourg will attest, it is not just mom and pop storefronts that are operating offshore; *the creme de la creme* are also in on the game. Among Luxembourg's hundreds of banks are a list of who's who in global finance: ABN Amro Bank, Bank of Bermuda, Bank of Tokyo, Banque de Gestion Edmond de Rothschild, Chase Manhattan Bank, Citibank, Deutsche Bank, Ing Bank, Lloyds Bank, and Union Bank of Switzerland.

The Bank of Nova Scotia (BNS), Canada's fourth largest bank, engages in more international business than any other Canadian bank and has set up branches in most of the Caribbean havens. Apparently, BNS anticipated limited growth potential in Canada, a country of only 30 million people, and determined that it's profits could be padded substantially by doing business offshore. Seems they were right.

Money is flooding into bank havens around the globe and BNS, along with other business savvy banks, has been there to greet the banzai sized waves of green bills looking to drop anchor offshore.

And, as illustrated below, there is no shortage of banks willing to provide a home for your funds:

▸ When walking down Bay Street in Nassau, The Bahamas, you will find a bank on virtually every corner - more than 400 at last count ... banks that is, not corners.

▸ On the immaculate streets of Luxembourg, the early morning aroma wafting in the air is not that of freshly baked bread but rather the scent of immense sums of money protected within the confines of more than 220 money houses.

▸ The upper-crust island nation of Jersey now counts up to 80 banks in its creditworthy stable.

▸ Bragging rights in the offshore finance industry belong to the biggest kid on the block, the fabled Cayman Islands, with more than 600 banks having fastened their golden vaults to the floors of high priced real estate in tropical Grand Cayman.

Other countries, such as Bermuda with only 3 banks, consistently rank among the first tier of bank havens but do not offer a wide array of financial institutions.

In the case of banks, however, quality is definitely more important than quantity. While Bermuda has only a small number of banks, each of them are well respected in international finance circles and can confidently point to balance sheets with assets in the range of several billions of dollars.

Evaluating Offshore Banks

When reviewing the merits of an offshore bank, pay close attention to the following factors:

- Financial strength
- Stable ownership and management
- Growth
- History of adherence to secrecy laws

A peaceful night's rest often means banking with one of the larger and well established institutions such as those listed on page 77 and others including, The Bank of Butterfield, Barclays Bank, Chase Manhattan, Coutts & Co., Credit Suisse, Midland Bank, Royal Bank of Canada, Royal Bank of Scotland, and Standard Chartered, to name just a few.

Still, some people prefer their funds to be held with a lesser known bank that operates only one branch located in a bank haven. The upside to the single branch bank is that the bank does not have any foreign based operations. Thus, it would be less likely to succumb to foreign government pressure to disclose client information, as outlined in Chapter 4.

The downside, which seems to outweigh the positives, is that the one pony bank usually has an asset base ranging from 5 to 50 million; puny in comparison with their multinational banking colleagues. A relatively small asset base negatively compromises stability in that one or two bad loans or investment decisions could wipe out the bank, and with it, your savings.

Also, these smaller banks are often family businesses. This should raise a red flag to fully investigate the competence of the management team and confirm that sufficient checks and balances are in place to deter any wrongdoing.

Accountability in the form of disclosure of information is extremely important from the perspective of an investor. If you come across any bank, large or small, that refuses to reveal their ownership structure or audited financial statements, you would be wise to keep your money away, far away, from that bank. If it smells rotten, then assume it is rotten, and run with your money to another bank.

Foreign Operations

Ideally, to enhance your privacy, find a bank that does not do business in your home country. Unfortunately, this cannot always be accomplished, especially for Americans. With the world gone global in the 1990s', it is nearly impossible to find a bank of any significance that does not operate from the United States.

Canadians will have an easier time finding a non-Canadian bank that does not carry on business in Toronto, the financial capital of Canada. Owing to anti-competitive banking laws that essentially seal the borders closed to foreign competition, the presence of foreign banks in Canada is severely restricted.

But, for Canadians, there is a positive to be found in this nearly closed market. With few foreign banks operating within this old British colony, the Canadian government would not have the same degree of leverage as that parlayed by the IRS in its skirmish with The Bank of Nova Scotia, as discussed in Chapter 4.

Still, the Canadian government has attempted to address the offshore issue. Presently, the taxman extends its jurisdictional reach beyond Canada by demanding that all offshore branches of Canadian financial institutions issue tax information slips for every client who is a Canadian resident.

Opening an Offshore Bank Account

The actual mechanics of setting up an offshore bank account are usually as simple as setting up an account at your local bank. An added advantage is that you do not have to visit the offshore bank to set up the account since documents may be delivered.

One notable exception includes several banks in The Bahamas. Certain banks insist that all persons who will be signing on the account *attend* at the bank before the account will be opened.

The Bahamas has a reputation as a haven for some of the world's drug cartels. Drugs are sold, cash is received, and then placed in a Bahamian bank account. The proceeds of crime are thus laundered by the unsuspecting Bahamian bank and, when the cash is withdrawn, it is *clean*. The intent of the personal appearance requirement, along with the presence of the U.S. Drug Enforcement Agency (DEA) which maintains a permanent office in Nassau, is to discourage drug dealers from laundering illicit proceeds through the Bahamian banking system.

The thinking is that if a personal visit to the bank is involved, the drug dealers will reduce their banking activity in The Bahamas to avoid the risk of being identified in person or by a video camera monitoring the bank.

Aside from some of The Bahamian banks, most other offshore countries allow for account opening documents to be completed at your advisor's office and then delivered to the bank. The following steps lead you through the process of opening a bank account:

▸ *Initial Contact*

A competent offshore advisor has relationships with several offshore banks and will provide all account documents and assistance necessary to complete the documents.

Bear in mind that some banks insist that customers be introduced by a reputable professional, usually an attorney, accountant, or bank manager. Even more restrictive, private banks that require large initial deposits, ranging from $200,000 to $500,000, demand an introduction from a professional *and* a personal visit from the individuals operating the account. When this much money is parked offshore, you too should want to get to know the banker who will be managing your funds.

The process of setting up an account may be more difficult if you bypass the assistance of an advisor. Depending on the bank, contacting a bank directly and requesting information about their services may meet with resistance.

This resistance results from domestic laws in certain countries, such as the United States, Canada, and Australia, which forbid foreign banks from soliciting business in their country unless they hold a bank license in, for example, the United States.

The definition of *soliciting business* has been interpreted to include something as simple as mailing an information package to a resident of those countries in question. For example, a bank in Guernsey, which is not licensed to operate in Canada, would likely be violating Canadian banking laws if it sent banking information to a Canadian address.

To side-step this barrier, arrange for the bank to send their information package to another country that does not prohibit foreign banks from *soliciting business* and then have the material forwarded to you from that country.

▸ **Completing The Documents**

If completing the documents without the assistance of a competent advisor then, before returning the documents to the bank, you may want to contact the bank to review the documents and ensure that they have been properly completed.

Although the completion of bank account opening

documents is not exactly the equivalent of brain surgery, you may mistakenly forget to cross the t's or dot the i's. And any mistake, no matter how minor, will delay opening of the bank account until properly completed documents are received by the bank. Whether offshore or onshore, flexibility is not a trait common to banks.

▸   ***Signatory***

One or more persons may sign on the bank account. As a matter of prudent estate planning, at least two people should have signing authority on the account. Where two people are on the account and one of the signatories dies, the other may continue operating the account without any interruption.

If, however, only one person is authorized on the account, what happens to the money when that person dies?

If no one else knows about the account then, eventually, the bank claims the money as its own. If your spouse knows of the account and attends at the bank to claim the money as your rightful heir, the bank will require proof of your death, proof that your estate has been probated, proof of your marriage to your spouse, proof of your spouse's identity, and proof that your spouse is entitled to the money.

In the worst case scenario, your spouse provides all of the above information but the bank still denies the claim of entitlement. If this were to happen, the remaining option would be for your spouse to petition the bank haven court to argue her claim. And there is no guarantee that the court would find in favor of your spouse.

Make it easy on your spouse or other heirs by authorizing the bank to accept instructions from one other person in addition to yourself.

> ### *Identification*

Reputable offshore banks require some form of identification for each person who will be signing on the account. A notarized copy of the photo and signature page of your passport is usually required although a notarized copy of your birth certificate and driver's license is sometimes accepted.

> ### *Letter of Reference*

A reference from another bank that you have been doing business with for at least 12 months will be required. Though some banks will accept a reference from another offshore bank, others will insist that the reference come from a bank that is located in your usual place of residence.

Some offshore banks allow for the reference letter to be addressed, "to whom it may concern" while others require that the name and address of the bank be included in the letter.

Certain banks require that the letter of reference be delivered with the account opening documents while others merely require you to provide the name and address of the referring bank. In this case, the offshore bank would then contact the referring bank to confirm that the reference is valid and that you have maintained your accounts in a responsible manner.

Banks insist that a reference be provided before an account is opened because, from the bank's perspective, they must protect themselves against criminal activity. Obtaining a bank reference, along with identification, is part of the bank's due diligence.

Other banks, usually private, will undertake a more comprehensive exercise in due diligence by requiring one or two additional references from an international law or accounting firm. Clearly, this will restrict the bank clientele to those people who retain the services of high-priced professionals.

Will these references compromise your privacy?

Yes, in the sense that you are revealing your personal information to an *offshore* bank. But this is the leap of faith that you take with an offshore bank - you assume that your business affairs will remain strictly private and that the risk of disclosure is minimal as long as you are not involved with serious criminal activities.

Remember that secrecy is the primary building block of the offshore finance industry. If one haven did not enforce client privacy, money would immediately take flight to another haven that respected and enforced confidentiality.

► **Delivery of Documents**

Use a courier such as DHL, Fedex, UPS or Purolator to deliver the documents to the bank. Sending the documents by regular mail is slow and risks the package being lost or opened by a prying postal employee or government agent. Sounds paranoid? Maybe. But this has happened in the past and may very well continue.

The following three examples lend a dose of credibility to this paranoia outbreak:

► The first episode took place in the 1970s. All mail sent from certain Swiss banks to residents of New York City was opened by government officials and a list of the intended recipients was compiled. A short time later, some of the intended recipients were alleged to have outstanding tax liabilities and were penalized.

This invasion of privacy could have been avoided by instructing the bank to either hold all mail or, rather than the mail being delivered directly to the New York City resident, have it delivered to the IBC's registered office, assuming that the account was in the name of an IBC.

▸ Example number two takes us north across the 49th parallel. In the late 1980s, the Canadian government surprised the back room of one of the largest banks in Canada with a nasty little raid on their Toronto office. This particular bank, like all of Canada's major banks, had offshore operations.

The zealous government agents were searching for client mailing lists and assumed that this information would be held in Toronto rather than in the offshore branches themselves. Fortunately for the bank and its clients, they were wrong.

▸ Today, it is not uncommon for Customs officials on both sides of the American-Canadian border to open and inspect mail.

▸ ***Initial Deposit***

Some offshore banks do not require any funds to be sent with the account opening documents. Others ask that a minimum sum, usually between $500 - $1,000, be deposited at the time that the account is opened. As previously mentioned, private banks will require that a significant sum be deposited before an account is opened.

More sophisticated banks allow for accounts to be held in several major currencies.

► *Is the Account Open Yet?*

The bank will review the account opening documents and then confirm the legitimacy of your banking reference and identification. Assuming everything is in order, the account may be open within 7 - 14 business days after receipt of the documents.

► *Operating The Account*

Once the account is up and running, written instructions are generally required to carry out transactions. These instructions may be delivered by fax or mail. For some banks, verbal instructions are not acceptable for the reason that the bank cannot identify your voice over the telephone but can verify your written signature.

If the bank is concerned about the authenticity of the signature on a fax, or if the bank is not comfortable with the instructions for some other reason, then they will insist that an original written instruction be delivered to the bank. Sure, this may be inconvenient but the bank is protecting you by ensuring that it is *your* signature on that piece of paper and not a forgery.

► **Codeword**

Ahhh, the *secret* codeword. This is the James Bond-like part of the game. Codewords are agreed upon between yourself and the bank at the time that the account is opened.

A significant percentage of banks ask that a codeword be quoted each time instructions are given. Acting as confirmation of identity, the codeword sometimes allows for verbal instructions to given. However, certain banks do not permit verbal instructions but require written instructions be given along with your signature and codeword.

One branch of a well known British bank has gone overboard with its codeword scheme. This branch requires that all instructions be given by fax and that a codeword be quoted on each written instruction. Okay, no problem yet. But this bank, requires that a whole *list* of codewords be submitted.

For the first transaction, you sign the instruction and quote codeword number one. For the second transaction, you sign the instruction and quote codeword number two. And so on down the list. If you have originally given a list of five codewords, once you reach codeword number five, you start again at one. Or, if you prefer to really complicate matters, you may submit a new list of codewords to the bank once you have exhausted one through five.

The reasoning behind this codeword mania is that, even if someone can accurately forge your signature, it is unlikely that they would know any of your codewords or the fact that the codeword is different with each transaction.

Another branch of the same bank that is *not* located offshore, requires a list of thirty codewords, each of which must be precisely five letters in length. The reasoning behind this brilliant set up ... "no comment," says the bank! It is absurd, to say the least.

While the bank's intentions are good, requiring too many codewords is overkill. Problems arise if you misplace your list of codewords or quote the wrong codeword for a particular transaction. This would delay carrying out transactions until the matter was resolved with the bank. One codeword ought to be sufficient.

◆

Your offshore account is now set up, your money has moved on over to the land of the confidential, and you sleep better at night knowing your assets are safely parked, locked, and you hold the only key.

Chapter 7

Offshore Investment Trading

◆

Now having an understanding of offshore banking, Maria resumed her questioning. Changing the topic to investment trading offshore, she put forth the following hypothetical situation:

"You know that I have been active in the stock markets during these past few years. Well, say that I am concerned that the once hibernating bears are grumbling a little too loud for my liking and I cash in some assets from the stock market. The proceeds are placed into a safe fixed term deposit in the offshore bank account of Silver Cap Holdings Corp.

But, believing in my magical powers to foresee the future, I look into my crystal ball and notice that the stock market downturn is only temporary. So, my money is locked up in the fixed term deposit for only 90 days. When the market bottoms out, I will withdraw the cash from the bank account and start buying up bargains. In anticipation of my jump back onto the financial market roller coaster, I want to set up an offshore investment account (OIA) to trade securities."

"Okay, first ..."

"Wait, one more point before you launch into your lecture. I do not want the OIA with the bank where Silver Cap does business. When I invest, I play by the rule of investment diversification. By the same token, I would not want all of my assets with one financial institution.

Now, before you tell me about the place where I might consider setting up an OIA, I have specific questions for you regarding the operations of an OIA."

Getting to Know OIAs

"Can an American or Canadian resident trade securities through an offshore investment firm?"

"Of course."

"In what type of securities may I invest?"

"Any security that could be purchased on the stock market through a domestic investment firm may be purchased via an offshore investment firm. And if you invest in foreign markets, keep in mind that you want to choose a firm that has access to investing in those foreign markets."

"Okay. What is the principal difference between an investment firm located in, say, San Francisco and one that operates from the Turks & Caicos Islands?"

"All other things being equal, the difference is geography. What I mean is that, as long as the Turks & Caicos Islands firm has adequate personnel, communications systems, and access to markets, it does not matter much from where the trade is made. You would make a phone call to your broker in Turks & Caicos Islands rather than your broker in San Francisco and the trade would be executed."

"If there is no difference between a local and an offshore firm, then why would I want to trade securities offshore?"

"The advantage cited most often is that an OIA offers privacy which cannot be secured domestically. If individuals want to keep their business confidential, they go offshore. Other reasons for setting up an OIA include potentially greater access to global markets and investment opportunities, and asset protection."

Where to Set up an OIA

"Alright" said Maria, "What about finding a reliable and trustworthy offshore investment firm. Where would I start? I mean, there are probably a million and one companies offering their services from tax havens and they will all claim to be reputable. How do I determine which ones reek of snake oil and which ones I can trust?"

"Well, the snake oil is sometimes difficult to distinguish from the real McCoy, no matter how experienced you are or how much knowledge you may have.

In this regard, a story circulating the office a few years ago concerned a group of wealthy businessman who were enticed to transfer several million dollars to a Middle Eastern investment firm. Apparently, the line which hooked the businessman was that their money would be safely invested in U.S. Treasury bills with a rate of return that was several times higher than the ordinary return.

Though the promised return was highly unusual and was not offered anywhere else, the businessmen chalked this up to the fact that they were the lucky few to fall into such a sweet deal. Seems that they had never heard of the phrase, IF IT SOUNDS TOO GOOD TO BE TRUE, IT PROBABLY IS.

Anyway, greed blinded the otherwise street smart businessmen from checking the background of the investment firm and the individuals with whom they were dealing and, unfortunately, they were scammed big time. The funds were transferred out from their accounts to the investment firm one day, and the next day the funds and the people on the receiving end of the money were no where to be found - no trace, no clue, nothing.

So you have to take precautions. At a minimum, pay heed to the following indicators:

▸ *Jurisdiction*

Choose a reputable tax haven that licenses and regulates investment firms, such as The Bahamas, Bermuda, Cayman Islands, Guernsey, Jersey, Luxembourg, Switzerland, or Turks & Caicos Islands.

Being resident in North America, you may want to lean toward the Caribbean countries for the simple reason that there will not be much of a time zone difference from Wall Street, if any.

Jersey, for example, is on London time which puts it five hours ahead of New York. Inconvenience arises when you need to get hold of your broker at 2:00 pm New York time but it is already 7:00 pm Jersey time and your broker is at the local tavern unwinding from a busy day's work.

▸ *Due Diligence*

After choosing a tax haven, the next step is to fully investigate the investment firms in that haven. Start by finding answers to the following questions:

How many years has the firm been in business? Who are the directors and major shareholders? Can you review the firm's financial statements for the past one to five years? Are they showing a healthy profit? What bank does the firm deal with and may you contact that bank for a reference? What is the dollar value of assets under management? Is the company service oriented, i.e., how quickly will your trade orders be executed? Is someone always available to take your order? Will you always be communicating with the same trader?

Once all of your questions are answered to your satisfaction, consider meeting with the people behind the investment firm and getting a first hand look at their operations. This will affect your level of comfort one way or another.

▸ *Liability Insurance*

The investment firm must have adequate investor liability insurance. For example, if you have $250,000 in equities resting in your account and the investment firm goes belly up, you want to be sure that your assets are covered by insurance. In other words, if you cannot recover your $250,000 from the investment firm, you will want to collect on the insurance policy or at least try and sue the insurance company for payment.

When confirming details of the firm's insurance policy, you should also confirm which company is providing the insurance coverage. A large insurance company is preferred, one which is not likely to go out of business any time soon.

▸ *Commission fees*

Commission fees should be on par with domestic full service firms in North America. Of course, the greater the value of assets in your OIA, the more power you have to negotiate lower commissions. You can always negotiate. If the firm is not willing to do so, you may want to find a more flexible company.

Fees will *not* be comparable to discount investment firms. Understand that you will pay a premium for going offshore and, for now, competition is not so cut-throat among offshore investment firms that they have to compete with the North American discount firms."

Opening & Operating an OIA

"I am one step ahead of you," I said to Maria. "Before you say anything, let me guess that you want me to move on to the actual operations of an OIA."

"Reading my mind like that, you must have gazed into my crystal ball!"

"Similar to an offshore bank, an offshore investment firm will typically require information about the IBC establishing the account and the individuals who will be authorized to trade on the account.

This information will include copies of identification, usually a passport, birth certificate or drivers license, of the shareholders of the company and possibly a bank reference for the shareholders.

Standard corporate account opening documents will be required. Your offshore advisor should assist with completion of these documents. Once executed, the documents may be delivered to the offshore investment firm via mail or courier, preferably courier for reasons of speed and security.

The account should then be opened shortly after receipt of documents. Once opened, you must have assets in the account before placing a buy order since trading on margin is often not acceptable since the firm does not care to take the risk of a client not settling their account.

The simplest method of transferring funds or securities *into* the account is by means of electronic transfer although bank drafts made payable to the IBC may be sent to the investment firm for deposit to the account. Once the assets are in the account, trading may begin. Transferring funds out of the account is done by instructing the investment firm to wire funds directly to your IBC's bank account. *(see Chapter 9 for a detailed discussion on confidential transfer of funds)*.

Trading orders are generally placed by telephone or fax. But, as a precautionary measure, you should make a record of the order placed just in case a dispute arises regarding the details of the order."

The Shady Side

"Getting back to the snake oil, you really have to beware of peddler's promoting "pot of gold at the end of the rainbow" investment opportunities. Sadly, there seem to be no shortage of con men, both onshore and offshore, who pitch their once in a lifetime opportunities to dreamers seeking a quick and easy buck.

On several occasions, different individuals have approached me asking for advice regarding these "fantastic investment opportunities." Each person presented a variation of the same investment scheme that was known by various names including the "Hi-Yield Program", or the "Bank Roll Program." I prefer to call it the "Find a Sucker and Rake in the Dough Program." Unfortunately, the scam sucks in too many participants who ultimately take a monetary bath.

It works like this:

The minimum investment is anywhere from $100,000 to $1,000,000.

You are "guaranteed" a minimum rate of return of 8% over a period of 90 days. Maximum return is unlimited. Typically, the investment promoter will tell about past clients who made upwards of 600% over a one year period. Ask him for the name of anyone so fortunate and you will hit a wall. No names will be revealed.

You will be told that the opportunity is exclusive, usually open only to "the top 25 banks in the world." For you, however, the window is open to join this cannot lose game but you must act fast. Gee, you are so lucky.

You will be given a few documents that will appear to be drafted by lawyers. You will also be given letters from banks and law firms, maybe legitimate, probably fraudulent, which attest to the authenticity of the investment.

Oddly, the promoters of these schemes often state that some prince or sultan from the Middle East is involved. For whatever reason, they seem to think that this lends credibility to the investment. While some may be impressed by being somehow associated with royalty, anyone with their eyes open should immediately be tipped off that the operation is a scam.

Some of these scam artists will return your money, without any interest, after 90 days. For these guys, the whole objective is not to rob you blind but to borrow large sums of someone else's cash, invest it for 90 days in Treasury Bills or some other safe investment, make some money, then return the principal.

The one's without any conscience at all will disappear along with all of your money.

I know of several investors, who became involved with one of these schemes and lost their proverbial shirt. What happened was this:

$500,000 was transferred to an offshore bank with the written promise that the funds would be held by an independent third party. The third party agreed not to release the funds without first receiving instructions from the investors.

After the money was sent, the investors were told that the first interest payment would be made within 90 days. 90 days came and went. Another 60 days passed by before the investors started to panic.

They were completely in the dark as to the whereabouts of their money and how to go about finding it. There was no one to contact since the promoter always called the investors but never left a number where he could be reached.

Eventually, the investors received a letter written on the letterhead of a prestigious Washington D.C. law firm. The letter was apparently signed by a senior partner of the firm.

The investors sent the letter to me and asked for comments. Well, I read the letter and it was a horrible piece of writing. I have had occasion to come across numerous examples of poor legal draftsmanship, but this letter was so awful that I refused to believe that it was written by a lawyer, let alone a $500/hr senior partner of a major law firm. The letter was clearly a fake that was written on stolen letterhead.

Now feeling desperate, fearing that they had lost all of their money, the investors clung to the belief that the letter was legitimate. It was not. And their money was gone.

If the investors had undertaken any due diligence on the people behind the investment scheme, I am sure that their bank account would still be full of money. But they did not do any checking. All that the investors saw was a phenomenal rate of return, a TOO GOOD TO BE TRUE rate of return, and they blindly transferred their money to someone whom they did not know.

Greed motivated the investors. Greed is foolhardy. In the end, greed loses."

Playing it Safe

If you come across one of these too good to be true investment opportunities, and you are tempted, go see a reputable attorney or accountant. Show them the documents. An hour or so of their time will be money well spent.

Chapter 8

SAFEGUARDING
YOUR PRIVACY

◆

Privacy has been big business ever since the year 1776 when a bunch of British chaps tossed aside the Union Jack in favor of the newly stitched Stars and Stripes.

Once this proud flag was anchored to American soil, the brightest legal and philosophical minds of the day assembled to pen some ground rules which would govern the nation's business. These rules were etched onto an historic document that would be known as the Bill of Rights. And one of the most important notions written on this roadmap to democracy was that of an individual's *right to privacy*.

But, intentionally or not, the Bill of Rights was not a clearly written document and, mere moments after the ink had dried, a line was drawn and sides were taken in a heated dispute centering around the breadth of the right to privacy. The cause of the dispute related to whether or not the right to privacy was *absolute*.

During the course of the new nations's first few hundred turbulent growing years, the Justices of the United States Supreme Court were called upon more than once to settle the disagreement one way or another. For the most part, the Justices decided that the right to privacy is not absolute.

Instead, the Justices recognized that a compromise must be reached between individual rights and the rights of the community in which we reside. Depending on circumstances, the priority would sometimes shift to the individual while at other times the community's interest would stand first in line.

Today, it remains clear that an individual's right to privacy is respected but, at times, must give way when other interests are more pressing. (At this point, I will end what is probably the most succinct, and surely not complete, overview of the "right to privacy" issue that you will ever come across!)

Breathing New Life into Privacy

As Big Brother continued to creep further into private lives, some countries saw an opportunity to create an industry built on the back of privacy. The opportunity existed in the form of crafting laws that put the *absolute* back into the right to privacy, at least when it came to financial interests.

The abundance of tax havens today is largely due to this assurance given by several countries to preserve financial privacy. And individuals who make use of tax havens take a leap of faith that the offshore institutions with whom they carry on business will keep their business affairs completely confidential.

Once this leap of faith is taken and your information is entrusted with an offshore institution, you should feel comfortable knowing that your privacy has been secured offshore. Now, your thoughts must turn to shielding your financial transactions from onshore prying eyes.

In this respect, your privacy concerns should focus on your activity back home, such as (i) how to communicate with your offshore financial institution in confidence; (ii) transferring funds offshore; and (iii) transferring funds onshore.

Just how far you want to go to ensure your privacy really depends on your risk behavior. Generally, there are three types of risk behaviors exhibited by individuals which are discussed below in the context of the "Caution Spectrum" (some call it the "Paranoia Horoscope"):

▸   ***Bunker Mentality***

You are sitting on the extreme right edge of the spectrum if you are radically risk averse, trust no one, believe that you are being followed everywhere you go, your conversations are wire-tapped, and "they" are out to get you.

▸   ***Prudently Cautious***

You stand in the middle of the spectrum if you are comfortable with a few loose ends, do not worry much about a few telephone calls to The Bahamas, and are not really hiding anything but just want your privacy.

▸   ***Break-Neck***

Spitting into the wind of caution, you thrive on risk and engage in activities like naked bungy jumping into the depths of the Grand Canyon and snowboarding Mt. Everest. Privacy? Relax! You are teetering on the far left of our little spectrum and may as well skip the rest of this chapter. For anyone else not into skydiving without a parachute, you might want to read on.

Confidential Communications

Communicating with an offshore financial institution will be carried out via telephone, facsimile, E-mail, snail mail (i.e., regular mail), or courier.

First, from the privacy angle, what is the problem with the telephone and facsimile? Well, a permanent record is kept of all telephone/facsimile calls including the time that the call was made, date, number dialled, duration of the call, and the location from which the call was placed. If you prefer that your home telephone line does not show calls placed to Monaco, a tax haven playground for the rich and famous, then do not call from home.

Still, if this is a concern, what do you do to dust up

the trail? The most effective option is to use a long distance telephone card. These are debit cards that allow you to purchase long distance calling time in advance. Since the cards are purchased anonymously, calls cannot be traced back to any individual when the call is made from a public phone.

Another option is to make the call from a location other than your home or office. Lastly, consider using a cellular phone that is not registered in your name.

The privacy alternatives for faxing documents include: sending a fax from a location other than your home or office; or sending and receiving faxes from your computer. Just remember to delete any record of the fax from the computer's hard drive once it is no longer needed. Re-formatting the hard drive every so often would also assist with eliminating any trace of the faxed information.

Additional precautionary measures include using codewords to identify yourself when speaking with your financial institution and removing the header which shows your name and number at the top of faxed communications.

Second on the mode of communication list is sending documents via the post office or courier. Mailing documents is slow and has a greater chance of being intercepted or lost while sending documents by courier is preferred since it is expedient and relatively safe. Couriered documents are tracked thus there are lower odds of a document disappearing.

Paying the courier with cash, rather than credit card, will avoid the package being traced back to you. As well, do not include your name or address on the sender's information part of the courier waybill.

Using E-mail over the Internet is the third way of communicating with offshore institutions. However, although the Internet offers convenience and by-passes long distance charges, individual privacy is not yet much of a concern in cyberspace and E-mail messages are not secure unless encrypted.

When travelling cyberspace, you are often marked and followed by a harmless sounding invader called a "cookie". No, not the chocolate chip variety. These cookies are intricate software programs installed by website operators and are used to store information about all travellers who visit the site.

They work like this: when you visit a website, your Internet browser is tagged with a cookie. The cookie then deposits itself into your computer. And while it remains fastened to the hardware innards, the cookie leaves a trail. Think of it as a homing device. From the spot where the cookie is dropped, your every move is followed and your route is relayed back to the cookie dropper. Though some cookies are erased when you shut down your browser software, others infect your hard drive for a lengthy period time, sometimes years.

The U.S. Federal Trade Commission is trying to implement legal restrictions which would restrict the use of cookies and other information collecting devices. But, until these restrictions are in place and shown to be effective, online privacy remains at risk.

To reduce this risk, consider installing (i) top grade encryption software to protect the privacy of your E-mail messages; and (ii) software that prevents you from being tagged with a cookie.

Transferring Funds Offshore

Several methods are available to transfer funds around the world but not all are conducive to securing privacy.

▸   *Wire Transfer*

Funds sent via wire transfer from a domestic institution to an offshore bank leaves an information trail showing the name of the receiving institution, name of the account holder, and account number to which the funds are transferred. Because domestic banks are, in some respects, government agents, information gleaned from a wire transfer will be available to the government or any other authority investigating your banking transactions.

Though not on the government payroll, banks remit interest income statements to the tax department and are legally obligated to report transactions involving large cash amounts or those transactions which appear to be suspicious.

In fairness, these reporting laws exist to discourage wrongful activities and are somewhat effective as a measure to combat money laundering. However, a side effect of tight regulations is an erosion of individual privacy that leads to others having access to your confidential information. This is an instance of the community interest taking precedence over individual rights.

Unfortunately, those who are given this right of access to an individual's private information do not always act fairly. In the following scenarios, two individuals were unfairly targeted by the government and, as a result, suffered financially. If these individuals had held some of their funds in an offshore bank account, then they may have held a stronger bargaining hand when trying to convince the government that their actions were not wrongful.

The first case took place in the fall of 1996 in small town Canada. Days after a woman's funeral, a government agency approached the deceased's family and requested repayment of pension money that was apparently paid to the deceased in error.

According to government records, the deceased died in the fall of 1995, not 1996. If this date were accurate, then the deceased's family wrongly received payments for more than one year since payments were intended to cease upon death.

Knowing that the government records were inaccurate, the family brought the original death certificate to the government agency. The year of death on the certificate was 1996.

For whatever reason, the agency refused to acknowledge the validity of the death certificate, insisted that the deceased died in 1995, and that payment was overdue. Not knowing what else to do, the family ignored the agency's repeated requests.

Several months passed by with no word from the agency. Apparently, they were busy locating the bank account of the deceased's husband. Once the account was found, the agency instructed the bank to release funds equivalent to the amount claimed owing by the agency.

The husband was infuriated when he learned that his account had been drained and demanded an explanation from the bank. The bank matter of factly stated that they had no choice but to comply; they could not refuse the request of this particular government agency.

The second example involves the Internal Revenue Service (IRS). Congressional hearings held in 1997 and 1998 that investigated the activities of the IRS revealed several instances of an abusive authority.

In one situation, a small businessman suffered through months of unjustified harassment from IRS employees who were seemingly determined to get their man.

Briefly, the IRS demanded payment of thousands of dollars for taxes allegedly owing. The businessman denied owing any money and refused to make payment. The IRS took action: liens were placed on his bank accounts, the effect of which was to freeze all funds in the account thereby preventing creditors from being paid.

Eventually, the creditors cut off goods and services from the businessman, he was unable to operate his business and declared bankruptcy. Months later, the IRS was shown to be in the wrong and an out of court settlement was reached.

▶ *Bank Draft / Money Order*

A money order or bank draft may be deposited into an offshore account but this method of transfer may jeopardize privacy. For example, when purchasing bank drafts, a local bank will usually ask for identification of the person purchasing the draft. The bank then records this information. When the offshore bank cashes the draft, it will not clear the account until confirmation of validity is received from the issuing bank.

When confirming validity, the issuing bank typically scans the draft into its computers. Remember that the draft will now have your signed endorsement on the back and will show to which bank and which account the draft is deposited. Your signature and the fact that you were noted by the issuing bank as the purchaser of the draft ties your name to the offshore account.

To reduce the risk of unwanted disclosure of information, consider purchasing a bank draft from a bank with whom you do not usually do business since an investigation of your financial affairs usually involves only your bank accounts.

► ***Personal Check***

Do not deposit a personal check from your local account into an offshore account if any semblance of privacy is your goal.

Like a bank draft, a check will be returned to the issuing bank to confirm that sufficient funds are in your account. The local bank then has on record the name of the bank and the account to which the check has been deposited.

What if someone else gives you a check drawn on their local account which is made payable to your IBC's account? Should you deposit this check to the offshore account? No, not if privacy matters.

As with a bank draft, the check would be sent to the issuing bank to clear. That bank would copy or scan the check and eventually return the check to the person on whose account the check was drawn. With your signature endorsement on the back, both the person who wrote the check and the issuing bank will know to which bank and which account the check was deposited.

▶   *Depositing Cash*

Cash does not leave a trail. But it is inconvenient, can be dangerous to carry, and even illegal depending on the amount carried and what borders you cross when transporting cash.

All banks have money laundering on the brain today. If you walk into a bank with $100,000, neatly stacked in $100 bills in your shiny briefcase, well, do not be surprised if the offshore bank shows you the door. A knock against their reputation is not worth a few dollars.

Offshore banks have a general policy to "know their customers". To smooth out a cash deposit, establish a relationship with the bank so that they know who you are and what type of business you are in. Once the bank is comfortable with you, let them know the source of the cash being deposited. The bank insists on knowing the source of funds to try to protect themselves from assisting with any sort of illegal activity.

Depositing cash amounts will incur a fee. This fee is often a percentage of the amount deposited, commonly around 0.05% of the total deposit.

▸   ***Third Party Source Transfer***

Risk of disclosure of information may be minimized where funds are transferred to an offshore account from a financial institution located *outside* of your home country.

In this instance, the funds would bypass your country of residence. The only record of the transfer would be held by the person arranging for the transfer of funds and the financial institution that completes the transfer. If you are comfortable with the third party, then this could be a secure method to transfer funds.

Transferring Funds Onshore

▸   ***Offshore Credit Card***

Plastic may be used to arrange for funds to come *directly* from an offshore bank to you. Many offshore banks issue credit cards, such as Visa, MasterCard or American Express. The currency of the credit card is usually denominated in U.S. dollars or British pounds.

Note that these are more like *debit* cards or *secured* credit cards. In other words, the bank will insist on taking security against your credit limit. For example, assume that you want a credit limit of $10,000. Most banks then require that you place $20,000 in a fixed term, interest bearing deposit. This secures the bank against the risk of you not paying the balance charged on the card. Typically, your credit line will be 50% of the amount placed in a fixed term deposit although some banks allow the credit line to be as much as 75% of the amount held as security.

Since the bank issuing the credit card is located in a tax haven, and assuming that secrecy laws are in force, all credit card transaction records will be confidential between the cardholder and the offshore bank. Thus, domestic credit bureaus will have no knowledge of your offshore credit card and your transaction history will not come up during a credit search.

Just like any other credit card, one issued from an offshore bank may be used to purchase goods or services as well as withdrawing cash from ATMs. If you do use the credit card for purchases, remember that the merchant from whom you purchase goods or services will have an imprint of the card which shows the name on the card and the account number. So, if you are not comfortable with this loose end, then use the card only for purchases made outside your country of residence.

When applying for the credit card, request that a PIN, i.e., personal identification number, be issued. The PIN will allow you to withdraw cash from Automatic Teller Machines (ATM) around the world.

▸ *Wire Transfer*

Upon your instruction some offshore banks will cloak their identity on the wire remittance form, as well as the name of the account and the account number. But it will still be possible to find out from which country the funds were sent. If requesting this of an offshore bank, be sure to explain that you merely want to keep your privacy intact. Otherwise, the bank may think that you are engaging in unwelcome activity, get nervous, and terminate its' relationship with you.

▸ *Picking up the Loot*

Travelling to the offshore bank, withdrawing cash, and bringing that cash back home with you is another option.

However, there are downsides to this route. First, there is the obvious risk of being robbed. Second, when you are returning home to or via the United States, and you are carrying $10,000 or more in cash or the equivalent amount in other negotiable commercial paper, such as share certificates, you are legally required to report this fact to the customs agent. Though the law does not prohibit you from carrying more than $10,000, you must be sure to disclose this fact. Otherwise, you are subject to severe penalties.

Presently, Canada does not have a similar disclosure law. This means that anyone may enter Canada with any amount of money and customs has no right to question or detain that person simply because they may carry a few million around in a briefcase.

Year after year, Canada is slammed by other countries as somewhat of a haven for criminals, and money launderers in particular. Lending support to this accusation is the fact that, of the 26 nations that comprise the Financial Action Task Force on Money Laundering, Canada is the only one that does not require the reporting of suspicious financial transactions to a central government agency.

Why is Canada the lone renegade? Only the politicians know the answer.

◆

In 1776, privacy concerns related to your neighbor peering through your window. Today, satellites orbiting the earth can pinpoint your precise location; video cameras follow you from the bank machine to the grocery store to the shopping mall and down the highway; and persistent little cookies track your moves in the virtual world.

For now, however, Big Brother has yet to invade the world of offshore finance.

Chapter 9

THE OFFSHORE TRUST

◆

If I wrote this entire book about offshore trusts it may very well have bored your pants off! I realize that the topic of trusts is not exactly a hot and sexy topic. Trusts do not have the broad appeal of a secret bank account with covert codewords nor the excitement surrounding offshore investment trading.

Rather, an offshore trust can be a difficult to understand and relatively expensive estate planning tool. With its' use typically restricted to those with assets in the $1,000,000 plus range, an offshore trust is not a commonly used vehicle.

Although it is not a realistic option available to everyone, there is still tremendous interest in learning about the possible benefits of a trust. Several times each week, I speak with people who are seeking information about offshore trusts and they ask questions something like this:

"What is a trust? Should I set up a trust? Can I avoid taxes? Protect my assets? Provide for my heirs? Is my portfolio large enough to justify the cost of setting one up? How much does it cost? Who should I use as a trustee? Will I retain any control over the assets? Where should the trust be set up?"

And on, and on, and on ...

It being such a broad topic, one chapter alone would not even come close to explaining the many uses of a trust nor the creative ways in which to tailor a trust to suit an individual's specific needs. To thoroughly exhaust this topic, a paper comparable in length to a long-winded Russian novel would have to be written and that would not be too exciting.

Still, a book about tax havens would not be complete without at least *some* discussion of trusts. So, I discuss the essential elements, the issues that you should know to provide yourself with a working knowledge of trusts.

If, during my attempts to entertain and enlighten, it so happens that I unintentionally bore your pants off, well, blame the nature of the subject for bringing on the *zzzzz's,* not me. Assuming you do remain awake throughout this chapter, once you make your way to the end, you should have an understanding of many of the fundamental issues related to an offshore trust. That, or a sure-fire cure for insomnia.

The Starting Point

The starting point was close to 1,000 years ago in jolly ole' England. During this time, owing to a desire to minimize tax bites and pass the silver spoon from one generation to the next, the *trust* was created. This new legal creature brought estate planning into *vogue* with royalty and the blue bloods.

Today, after ten centuries of evolution, the trust concept is little changed. Plain and simple, a trust remains an estate planning vehicle; flexible enough to accommodate a variety of needs including, asset protection, asset management, preservation of family wealth, legal avoidance or deferral of probate taxes, inheritance taxes and other forms of taxation, financial support of dependents, and enhancing financial privacy.

▸ *So, What is a Trust?*

A trust refers to a *relationship* between several persons. Unlike a company, a trust is not a separate legal entity.

▸ *Well, is a Trust Registered, like a Company?*

Not necessarily. The trust relationship is private between the people involved with the trust and it may not be necessary to register the trust with a government agency. Even though an official registry may not exist and the trust is not registered, it is a relationship that is recognized and enforced by law.

▸ *If it's not Registered, How do You Prove its Existence?*

The trust relationship is usually ascertained by a written document, known as a "trust deed," "settlement deed," "trust instrument" or "declaration of trust" - each of these terms having essentially the same meaning. It is the trust deed that details the terms and conditions that govern the relationship between the parties to the trust. Throughout this Chapter, for simplicity's sake, this document will be referred to as a *trust deed*.

Parties to the Trust

There are three principal parties, each of whom may be an individual or a corporation, who are involved with a trust:

▸   The *settlor* transfers legal title of their own property to the trust.

▸   The *trustee* holds *legal* ownership of the property which was transferred by the settlor.

▸   The *beneficiary* holds *beneficial* ownership of the same property.

The Settlor

"How about dropping the legal terms and explaining to me what it really means to be a settlor, trustee or beneficiary," said Maria.

"Okay. Imagine that your father, Antonio, is interested in setting up a trust for the purpose of providing financial security for you and your sister and your sister's two children. If Antonio is the one who is setting up the trust, then he would be the settlor and his children and grandchildren would be the beneficiaries.

Say that Antonio arranges to transfer $150,000 cash, held in several fixed term deposits, and a securities portfolio with a present market value of $550,000 (together referred to as the "property") to the trust.

Once the trust deed and other required documents are signed, title to the property is transferred to the trustee. I will call the trustee Haven Trust Co. ("HavenTrust").

Once the property is transferred, Antonio no longer owns the property. HavenTrust is now the legal owner of the property and is now responsible for managing the property for the benefit of the children and grandchildren.

Assuming that Antonio's trust is an *irrevocable* trust, this means that, once the trust is established, Antonio may not revoke the trust and reclaim ownership of the property. On the flip side, if the trust was *revocable*, then HavenTrust would be obligated to return the property upon Antonio's request."

The Trustee

"HavenTrust, as the trustee, is responsible for managing and administering the property. Importantly, while HavenTrust holds legal title to the property, it does not have any right to personally use this property. If HavenTrust wrongfully used the property, it could be fired as trustee and sued if any damage were done to the property.

When exploring the possibility of establishing a trust, the most common concern that people have is the role of the trustee. In this case, Antonio might be concerned that HavenTrust will be the owner of his assets.

This concern is perfectly understandable. Handing over control of your assets to another person is a difficult matter, regardless of the legal obligations imposed upon the trustee. Some people just will not do it and, as a result, choose not to set up a trust."

"Let me understand this," said Maria. "You are saying that Antonio would transfer legal ownership of his property to HavenTrust, a company with whom he has never met?"

"Yes."

"And that Antonio will no longer own the property once it is transferred. The trustee will hold legal title to his property?"

"That's right."

"Well, that sure makes me uneasy and I would think that Antonio would not be too comfortable either. I mean, who is HavenTrust? How can we trust someone whom we do not know? What assurance do we have that HavenTrust will not run off with Antonio's property?"

"Well, the answers to your questions depend on several factors. First, Antonio has to feel comfortable with HavenTrust. And finding that level of comfort may be a different process for everyone.

For example, one of my clients insisted on using the trust arm of Union Bank of Switzerland (UBS), presently the third largest banking group in the world. He wanted UBS precisely because of their size, their reputation, their track record, and the fact that these factors together added up to a lower risk that his property would be mishandled, inadvertently or not.

But before taking the plunge and making the decision to use UBS, other factors had to be considered to assist my client with finding his level of comfort with UBS, including the following:

▸ Does the trustee operate from a well regulated jurisdiction with established trust laws, such as the Cayman Islands, the Cook Islands, The Bahamas, or Bermuda.

▸   Is the trustee required to pay taxes on the property held in trust?

▸   For how long has the trustee been in business?

▸   What is the value of assets held under management by the trustee?

▸   Does the trustee carry liability insurance on your property for a value at least twice its market value?

▸   Is the liability insurance policy with a reputable and well known insurance company?

▸   Is the trustee subject to an annual audit by an accounting firm of international repute?

▸   Will the trustee freely disclose their audited financial statements to you?

▸   Have you met with the trustee and are you comfortable with the people who will be managing your property?"

"Okay." said Maria.   "Let's say that HavenTrust meets all of your criteria. Call me crazy but I would still have a problem with giving my property to someone who I really do not know. What if Antonio were to use his brother as the trustee? Could he do that?"

"Yes. Having a relative act as a trustee is common. But, there are downsides including the following:

▸   For one thing, Antonio's brother is a resident of Canada. This means that the trust property would be subject to Canadian tax rates, which are horrendously high.

▸   Second, his brother is not a professional money manager. What if he mismanages the property and its value decreases? Would your family sue him for failing in his duties as trustee even though his mismanagement was not intentional?

▸   Third, even if Antonio's brother does have a head for the stock markets, what if he is too busy with his own business affairs and does not have enough time to properly manage the property and make all of the required investment decisions?

▸   Fourth, what happens if his brother dies and the property has not been fully distributed to you, your sister, and her children? Who would take over his duties? Sure, at the time that the trust is set up, I could anticipate this event by arranging for another person to act as trustee, but what if that person also dies either before your brother or shortly after? How many alternative trustees should we consider?

Those are some of the downsides to having an individual act as trustee. Now, while the same level of comfort may not be present with a corporate trustee as would be with Antonio's brother, some of the potential pitfalls just mentioned could be overcome by using a corporate trustee, such as HavenTrust:

▸ Being resident in the Turks & Caicos Islands, HavenTrust is not subject to pay taxes on any of the trust property.

▸ If the property substantially decreases in value because of mismanagement by HavenTrust, then HavenTrust and its insurance company could be sued.

▸ HavenTrust is hired to take care of your property. Since that is their only business, Antonio should not have to worry about HavenTrust having time to properly fulfill their responsibilities.

▸ Death of HavenTrust is less likely to be an issue since it has a history of solid finances and sound management practices. Reviewing HavenTrust's financial statements on a regular basis would allow you to quickly transfer the property elsewhere if you learned of any impending financial problems."

The Beneficiary

"You, your sister, and her children would be the beneficiaries of the trust. As beneficiaries, you are the only people entitled to use the trust property. An important caveat here, however, is that the beneficiaries entitlement to use of the property kicks in only *after* the property has been distributed; the property is distributed in accordance with the terms of the trust deed.

So, while the property remains in trust, the beneficiaries have no right to its use. In legal jargon, the beneficiaries have what is known as a *contingent* interest in the trust during the time that the trust property remains with the trustee.

As an example assume that, according to the terms of Antonio's trust, your niece and nephew will receive $3,000 per month once they reach the age of 18, but only if they pursue a university education. Presently, the children are in junior high school so their interest in the trust is contingent in that they have not yet received anything from the trust and will not receive anything until they reach the age of 18 and attend university.

Once they reach 18 and start their post-secondary studies, their interest will be said to have *vested*; meaning that the monthly payments will now be distributed to them.

For each of the beneficiaries, during the time that they hold a contingent interest, they still have certain rights with regard to the property. For example, since HavenTrust is managing the property for the benefit of you and members of your family, you may take legal action against HavenTrust if they fail to adequately perform their duties, such as maintaining the value of the trust property. These duties will be spelled out in the trust deed. Typically, all trust deeds should include the right to sue the trustee for failure of obligations owed to the beneficiaries."

The Trust Deed

"The trust deed is the fundamental document which spells out the terms of the trust, such as: the name of the settlor; appointment of the trustee; identification of the beneficiary; a detailed description of the property to be transferred to the trust; the duties, responsibilities, and powers of the trustee; and the terms upon which the property is to be distributed to the beneficiary.

The terms of the trust deed should be tailored to your specific circumstances to provide you with maximum asset protection and other estate planning advantages."

May the Settlor Retain Control?

"Earlier, you emphasized the difference between an irrevocable and a revocable trust. If the trust is irrevocable, does this mean that Antonio is completely out of the picture once he transfers his assets over to HavenTrust?"

"No. To a certain degree, Antonio may be indirectly involved with the administration of the trust. Just how much involvement is allowed is an issue determined by the specific facts. However, the general rule is that, for a trust to be valid, the trustee must retain control of the property, *both in form and in substance*.

One scenario which would allow Antonio to keep his nose in HavenTrust's business involves using an IBC as a holding company for the trust property. Typically, one or more IBCs are set up to hold trust property. This provides an additional measure of anonymity with regard to the operation of the trust as well as asset protection since the assets are held by a limited company rather than an individual.

In this scenario, HavenTrust would be the 100% owner of the IBC while the board of directors and officers of the IBC may include HavenTrust and other persons.

Now, this is where it gets a bit tricky: Antonio, his lawyer, another family member or friend, may be appointed as an officer or director of the IBC. For this example, say that Antonio is appointed to the office of assistant treasurer of the IBC. Not exactly a prestigious or highly visible position but titles do not always tell the whole story.

If you look closely at the bylaws of the IBC, it becomes clear that all corporate decisions must be arrived at through unanimous consent of *all* officers. This means that no decision may be approved without the consent of Antonio, the lowly assistant treasurer. The effect of the IBC bylaws has been to provide Antonio with the power to pass or veto any proposed corporate actions.

Would this structure wash?

Well, if it's legitimacy were challenged in court, the thrust of any challenge would be to the validity of the trust itself. It would be argued that HavenTrust does not have sufficient control over the administration of the trust. In deciding this argument, all of the circumstances surrounding the operation of the trust would have to be considered.

If, for example, Antonio, as assistant treasurer of the IBC, blocked every action with which he did not agree, and HavenTrust was the lone dissenter on each of these proposed actions, then a strong argument could be put forward that the trust is invalid. In this case, it would be apparent that Antonio was actually controlling the IBC, and, by extension, the trust."

► ***Protector***

"Appointing a *protector* may also give Antonio some indirect control over the trust."

"What is a protector?" asked Maria.

"A protector, who is commonly involved with an offshore trust, may be an individual or a corporation. As the name says, a protector acts to *protect* the interests of the beneficiaries and to keep a watchful eye on the trustee to make sure that they properly carry out their responsibilities.

Antonio would appoint someone close to him, such as a family member or trusted advisor, to act as the protector of the trust. Because the protector is someone close to Antonio, he would likely have some indirect influence over the protector and therefore the trust.

The powers of the protector would include the power to review some of the proposed actions of HavenTrust and the right to veto some, but not all, of HavenTrust's proposed actions. In certain situations, the protector may hold the right to remove HavenTrust and arrange for the appointment of a new trustee. However, though the protector's powers may be generous, they may not be so significant as to wrest control of the trust away from HavenTrust.

How do you know if the protector has too *much* power? That is a question that can be answered only by reviewing the trust deed and the actions taken by the protector during the administration of the trust. But keep in mind that it is usually better to err on the side of caution so as not to give the protector so much control that the validity of the trust is at risk."

▸   *Wish Upon a Trust*

"A third method that may be used by Antonio to retain indirect control over administration of the trust involves a document known as a *letter of wishes*.

Usually written at the same time as the trust deed, the letter of wishes would include statements by Antonio which suggest that certain actions be carried out by HavenTrust. These actions would relate to matters that could not be anticipated at the time that the trust was set up, such as adding or removing certain beneficiaries.

In anticipation that other matters may arise *during* the life of the trust, but *after* the trust is settled, Antonio's letter of wishes may also be used to provide that another person, such as his wife, should have the right to submit additional letters of wishes to the trustee. Antonio's wife would take on this role since the trust is *irrevocable* and Antonio is not allowed to provide a letter of wishes after the trust is set up.

Let me illustrate the possible use of a letter of wishes:

Say that a few years have passed by and your sister's children are now 18 and 19, respectively. The 19 year old's interest in the trust has vested. She is enrolled in a pre-dentistry program at Colgate University and is receiving her $3,000 per month trust distribution.

The 18 year old, well, he too pursued higher education. Mind you, a different sort of higher education. One in which "high" appears to be the central theme. He is enrolled in a liberal arts program at Flounders U. where he is an active member of the Friends of Outer Space Society and is donating upwards of $1,000 per month to them; money taken from his monthly trust distribution.

Antonio would like to immediately suspend all trust payments until his grandson straightens out and suggests that his wife write a letter of wishes to HavenTrust which would say something similar to the following:

"This letter is not intended to impose any legally binding obligation upon you, fetter your discretion in any way, or create any enforceable rights for any of the beneficiaries, but rather is intended to suggest that you consider the following circumstances ... "

The letter of wishes would continue by referring to

the terms of trust deed which make reference to the distributions to be made to his grandson and would then suggest, not demand, but merely suggest, that these terms be amended or not followed precisely as written. New terms would then be suggested.

It is important to understand that although the letter of wishes is a persuasive document, it does not technically force the hand of HavenTrust. While a letter of wishes is meant to be influential, it is not legally binding upon HavenTrust, meaning that HavenTrust is not under any obligation to follow the suggestions put forth in the letter of wishes. In practice, however, HavenTrust would carry out the suggestions stated in the letter of wishes as long as they would not be exposing themselves to undue risk of liability.

Remember that HavenTrust must maintain a sufficient degree of control over the management of the trust property. Otherwise, there would be no trust and the relationship between the various parties would be a sham.

Why?

Because, in such circumstances, HavenTrust would be a mere dummy figure that does not actually have any decision making powers. This would be completely contrary to the true purpose of a trustee."

My Trust Is Where?

Water cooler dialogue goes something like this:

"No, no, a Cook Islands trust is the best."

"Well, I heard that you cannot beat a Bahamas trust for asset protection."

Then a third "know it all" pipes in, "Okay, but if you want a trust that lasts a really long time, then Belize is the place to be."

These water cooler guys, whether they know it or not, are talking about what *laws* should apply to a trust. The trust deed will have a separate paragraph that specifically names the country whose laws will govern the trust. If desired, it is possible for different terms of the trust to be governed by the laws of more than one country. But regardless of which countries' laws apply to the trust, the trust property may be located in any country chosen by the trustee.

For example, an IBC which acts as the holding company for a trust that is governed by the laws of Belize may maintain a bank account in Bermuda, manage an investment trading account through a brokerage firm in the Cayman Islands, operate a second bank account from the Isle of Man, and own a condominium in Florida.

So which country offers the *best* trust laws? The answer to this question really depends on your specific circumstances and the purpose for which the trust is established.

For example, if you set up a trust for the sole purpose of protecting your assets, then the Cook Islands may be your choice. The laws of the Cook Islands are well known for making the lives of creditors extremely difficult.

Keep in mind that, owing to the intensely competitive nature of the offshore trust business, any tax haven country with a few bucks in its advertising budget will promote its own laws as "the best." This is an industry worth literally billions and billions of dollars and countries will do what they can to attract business.

To find the tax haven that best suits your needs, undertake your own research and consult with an experienced offshore trusts lawyer who can properly advise you. Only a competent lawyer will understand the laws of the countries relevant to your trust.

You would be foolish to entrust your hard earned assets to an offshore snake oil salesman who can offer you little except a bargain basement fee. The preservation, security and growth of your assets are much more important than saving a few pesos on set up fees.

You know the saying, an ounce of prevention is worth a pound of cure? Well, take it to heart if you set up a trust and go see a lawyer.

Speaking of Fees ...

With a reputable trustee, you are looking at a rock bottom minimum of about $3,000 to set up a trust and a $1,500 minimum annual fee to maintain it. Rather than a fixed fee, annual fees are often based on a percentage of the value of the assets held in trust. For example, if you have $1,500,000 in trust, then anywhere from 0.5% to 3% of those assets would be the trustee's annual fee.

You will find an enormous price range out there. I have seen quotes ranging from $400 to $40,000! What's going on? Why the significant discrepancy? What are you getting for $40,000 that you are not getting for $400?

To start with, $400 is nonsense. Any clown charging $400 is simply baiting you with ridiculously low fees. They do not actually set up a trust for you. Instead, they provide you with a standard boilerplate trust deed and you fill in the blanks, e.g., name, address. You are not provided with proper legal advice and the trustee may or may not actually exist! It is a waste of time and money dealing with slippery conmen who are in the game only for a quick dishonest buck.

On the other hand, anyone charging $40,000 is either robbing the ill-informed blind or is a large trust company or international accounting or law firm charging their wealthy clients a premium. They justify the premium on the basis that:

▸   The client has a thick billfold and is willing to pay for the prestige of being a client of XYZ firm.

▸   The client knows nothing about offshore matters, including cost and value.

▸   The client wrongly believes that the more that you pay, the better value received. Merchants just love people like that!

A more reasonable cost for a trust ranges between $3,500 to $6,000. You, as the buyer of services, have the responsibility to beware. Serious effort should be invested in shopping around for a reasonably priced and reputable advisor who can properly assist with your offshore trust.

Naming the Trust

Although a trust may be set up for one or more purposes, several of which are noted on page 126, it is the primary purpose of the trust that will commonly determine its name.

For example, a trust which specifically addresses the issue of asset protection is commonly referred to as an Asset Protection Trust (APT); a Family Trust is established for the benefit of the settlor's relatives; and a Discretionary Trust is one which gives discretion to the trustee to decide how both the income and capital of the trust property is to be distributed to the beneficiaries. Regardless of the name, a trust is a trust is a trust.

The Asset Protection Trust (APT)

One type of trust which will be discussed in some detail is the APT.

Owing to the excessively litigious nature of our society, asset protection seems to be the most prevalent reason for setting up an offshore trust. The APT is installed to combat the possibility of winding up on the losing end of a wrongful lawsuit. Properly crafted, the APT acts as an airtight insurance policy that fiercely protects your property.

Typically, those who have ongoing business contact with the public, such as professionals, directors and officers of companies, business persons, and other high net worth individuals, set up an APT. Because these people have money, they may be easy targets for creditors and overzealous lawyers looking for a *deep-pocket* defendant.

▸   *Assets Transferred to the APT*

Assets given the highest level of protection within the APT are those known as *intangible* assets, i.e., stocks, bonds and other commercial paper, including cash.

This high level protection shifts into gear when the intangible assets are held by a financial institution located in a tax haven country that strictly adheres to secrecy laws. Of course, any attempt to gain access to these assets would be frustrated by the secrecy laws that generally prohibit releasing any information without the client's consent.

Tangible assets, i.e., house, yacht, automobile, may also be transferred to the APT. However, unlike intangibles, tangible assets will be governed by the laws of the jurisdiction where the asset is located. For example, in the event of a successful court challenge against a trust where the complainant contested the rightful ownership of title to real estate located in North Carolina, a North Carolina State court would ultimately have the power to disregard the trust - simply because the real estate is located in North Carolina - and award the real estate to the person who contested the trust. The fact that the trust was otherwise governed by the laws of a tax haven country would be irrelevant.

▸   *Firewall*

For assets that are held in tax haven countries, any

creditor would face tremendous financial and procedural hurdles when attempting to track down assets held in the APT.

Remember that, if you are sued, there are essentially two objectives to the legal process. First, win the lawsuit. Second, assuming that you win then you become the creditor and the loser of the lawsuit becomes the debtor. Now, you have to collect the court award from the debtor.

If the debtor refuses to pay the court award, then you have to pursue other legal options in order to collect the award. This may be difficult if the debtor's assets are fit snugly within an APT.

If an APT had been set up *before* the lawsuit began and ownership of most, if not all, of the debtor's assets were transferred to it then, practically speaking, those assets would be out of your reach. In this scenario, at a minimum, the debtor would be in an extremely effective bargaining position for any settlement negotiations.

As discussed on page 150, an APT may not be effective if assets are transferred *after* the lawsuit began.

▸   *Antonio's Firewall*

"How about putting this APT vehicle in perspective by running through an example?" asked Maria.

"Sure. Assume that Antonio, transferred some of his assets to an APT in January, 1998. HavenTrust, the trustee, now legally owns the assets.

In June, 2001, a bitter ex-business partner, Casey, obtains a court order against Antonio in a United States court of law. Antonio refuses to pay the court award because he claims to have lost the case on an unfair technicality.

During the course of trying to determine whether Antonio owns any assets of value, Casey's lawyer hears through the grapevine that Antonio set up an offshore trust with a trustee named HavenTrust in the Turks & Caicos Islands. Going on the assumption that anyone who has an offshore trust probably has substantial assets, the lawyer wants to follow up on this piece of gossip and find out whether it is true. But the lawyer's information is limited. A few important matters that he definitely does not know are that:

▸   The trust is governed by the laws of Belize.

▸   Title to the assets is held by 3 different IBCs.

▸   The assets are located in 4 different jurisdictions. None are in Belize and less than $1,000 is held in a bank account in the Turks & Caicos Islands. (This account is simply used to pay expenses incurred by HavenTrust).

▸   To find out more information, Casey's lawyer

decides to contact HavenTrust.

Before continuing with my story, let me add that the date on which the trust was established, January, 1998, and the date of the court order, June, 2001, are both important dates for reasons I will now explain.

Most tax havens have built into their trust legislation a provision that discusses the issue of *fraudulent conveyances*. Briefly, a trust may be determined to be invalid if assets were fraudulently conveyed, i.e., transferred with the knowledge and intent to defraud a creditor or potential creditor.

If Antonio transferred his assets to the trust *after* Casey obtained the court order, or at any point after the lawsuit began, then it is quite possible that the trust would be found to be invalid by a court of law. The result being that Casey could obtain the right to seize the trust property in satisfaction of payment of the court award.

The leading offshore trust jurisdictions generally provide that assets transferred to a trust are protected from a claim of fraudulent conveyance if they have been in trust for a certain period of time, usually 1 to 3 years. This means any court action based on a claim of fraudulent conveyance must be commenced within the applicable time period.

So, for example, if the time period is *2* years, and the challenge to the validity of the trust is started *3* years after the trust was set up, then a claim of fraudulent conveyance will not succeed because the time period starts ticking from the date that the trust is established.

As a settlor shopping for the appropriate APT haven, the time limitation period is an essential consideration. From the perspective of Antonio, the shorter the limitation period the better.

Okay, back to my story:

Before his lawyer contacts HavenTrust, Casey decides to take over and calls HavenTrust, threatening to sue if they do not release information about the trust. HavenTrust remains tight-lipped and rejects Casey's demands to provide information concerning Antonio, including refusing to confirm or deny that Antonio has actually set up a trust.

By its actions, HavenTrust is simply fulfilling its legal responsibility *not* to disclose any information to Casey nor to any other person who does not have an interest in the trust.

Casey then thinks that he will have better results if he visits Turks & Caicos Islands and applies pressure to HavenTrust or whoever else may be holding the trust property. He reasons that because HavenTrust is in Turks & Caicos Islands, then it is likely that some of the trust funds are held with a bank or investment company in Turks & Caicos Islands.

Since he has no contacts in Turks & Caicos Islands, Casey hires a private investigator (PI) to snoop around the financial institutions on the island. But, to his dismay, the PI cannot break through the secrecy laws. Even if the PI could bribe a bank employee to check names of the account holders, the PI would not find any helpful information. Remember that the assets are held by three different IBCs and Casey does not know the names of the IBCs nor the names of the persons authorized to sign on the bank accounts.

At this point, Casey is becoming increasingly frustrated. He has spent thousands of dollars to obtain the court order in the United States. Thousands more have been spent flying to Turks & Caicos Islands, hiring the PI, lodging, food and lots of booze to calm his increasingly frazzled nerves. As well, he has taken time off from work at home, thus foregoing his usual income. As his frustration increases, his blood pressure rises, and his family urges him to cut his losses and come back home.

But Casey is persistent and not yet ready to throw in the towel. He thinks that if the Swiss banks can be persuaded to open up their banking books a little bit, then he can surely pry some information loose from Turks & Caicos Islands.

Unfortunately for Casey, he fails to understand that his situation is not even remotely similar to the Swiss scenario. He glosses over the fact that: (i) he does not have the bulk of highly placed politicians and businesspeople behind him to apply pressure on HavenTrust or the Turks & Caicos Islands government; (ii) he has no political connections; and (iii) no one other than Casey and his lawyer really care much about his claim.

Still, Casey soldiers on. He proceeds to meet with a lawyer in Turks & Caicos Islands and instructs him to bring a new court action.

Although many countries have what is known as Reciprocal Enforcement of Judgments legislation - this means that a judgment in one country may be recognized and enforced in another country - Turks & Caicos Islands does not recognize foreign court orders. So, to enforce his claim, Casey would have to start a new lawsuit in the Turks & Caicos Islands courts. This would mean thousands more dollars in legal fees and related expenses and, with the wheels of justice moving awfully slow in the Caribbean, it will be a long time before Casey's lawsuit even comes to trial.

Add to this the fact that the Turks & Caicos Islands lawyer tells Casey that even if he brought a new lawsuit in the local courts and won, it is unlikely that Casey would collect any money from Antonio. This is because there is likely a *flight provision* in the trust deed. This means that there is a clause in the trust deed that allows HavenTrust to move the property held in trust to another country if they determine that such a move would be beneficial for the trust.

Odds are that, upon learning that a legal challenge would be made against the trust, HavenTrust would relocate whatever property remained in Turks & Caicos Islands to another jurisdiction, and Casey would have to chase Antonio through the courts of another country.

At this point, Casey would be financially and emotionally drained and would probably end his pursuit of Antonio."

◆

"You know," started Maria, "The APT and the rest of the offshore business that you have been rambling on about really does not seem so mysterious anymore. I mean, until now, I have not bothered to ask you about this stuff but from listening to other people, I thought there was some kind of magic involved with going offshore."

I replied, "Well, the mystery tends to disappear once you have the knowledge. And with that knowledge, you are able to make an informed decision as to whether you would benefit from taking some of your business offshore."

EPILOGUE

◆

I write a book about tax havens and the subject of taxes is barely touched upon? Well, the title could have rightfully been called, "The *Financial* Haven Guide Book" since the topics of discussion have more to do with taking care of finances rather than taxes. But, with *tax havens* being such a well known term, I decided to stick with the tried and true.

It was intentional on my part not to discuss the issue of taxation. A number of reasons led me to this decision: (i) for both American and Canadian taxpayers, there are some excellent books sitting in the bookstores that provide a detailed discussion of tax issues as they relate to offshore structures - I did not want to repeat information that is already available to the reader; (ii) this book was intended to provide the reader with the *how to, where to, and why to* of going offshore, the intention was not to educate about tax laws; (iii) tax laws change so rapidly that by the time this book was published, the tax information could be inaccurate as a result of changes to the tax laws; and (iv) just as an offshore structure is tailored to an individual's specific needs, the tax implications of each offshore structure may be different for each individual.

That said, I would be doing an injustice to each reader if I did not mention the following: TAX ISSUES MUST BE CONSIDERED BEFORE SETTING UP ANY OFFSHORE STRUCTURE.